THE SURVIVAL GUIDE FOR

Kids in
Special
Education
(And Their Parents)

Understanding What Special Ed Is
& How It Can Help You

Wendy L. Moss, Ph.D.
Denise M. Campbell, M.S.

free spirit
PUBLISHING®

Library of Congress Cataloging-in-Publication Data
Names: Moss, Wendy (Wendy L.), author. | Campbell, Denise M., 1969– author.
Title: The survival guide for kids in special education (and their parents) : understanding what special ed is & how it can help you / by Wendy L. Moss, Ph.D., and Denise M. Campbell, M.S.
Description: Minneapolis, MN : Free Spirit Publishing Inc., [2017] | Includes index. | Audience: "Interest Level Ages: 8–14"—T.p. verso.
Identifiers: LCCN 2016048604 (print) | LCCN 2017002281 (ebook) | ISBN 9781631981678 (Paperback) | ISBN 1631981676 (Paperback) | ISBN 9781631981685 (Web PDF) | ISBN 9781631981692 (ePub)
Subjects: LCSH: Learning disabled children—Education—United States—Juvenile literature. | Special education—United | Special education—Parent participation—United States.
Classification: LCC LC4704.73 .M67 2017 (print) | LCC LC4704.73 (ebook) | DDC 371.9—dc23
LC record available at https://lccn.loc.gov/2016048604

Free Spirit Publishing does not have control over or assume responsibility for author or third-party websites and their content. At the time of this book's publication, all facts and figures cited within are the most current available. All website URLs are accurate and active; all publications, organizations, websites, and other resources exist as described in this book; and all have been verified as of January 2017. If you find an error or believe that a resource listed here is not as described, please contact Free Spirit Publishing.

Reading Level Grade 6; Interest Level Ages 8–14;
Fountas & Pinnell Guided Reading Level W

Edited by Alison Behnke
Cover and interior design by Colleen Rollins, production by Emily Dyer
Illustrations by Ann Kronheimer

10 9 8 7 6 5 4 3 2 1
Printed in the United States of America
V20300117

Free Spirit Publishing Inc.
6325 Sandburg Road, Suite 100
Minneapolis, MN 55427-3674
(612) 338-2068
help4kids@freespirit.com
www.freespirit.com

FSC
www.fsc.org
MIX
Paper from
responsible sources
FSC® C005010

Dedicated to my family members and dear friends, each of whom have enriched me in their unique and special ways. I am fortunate to have you in my life! I also dedicate this book to the many students who have learned to have the courage to be confident, build on strengths, and accept help to deal with difficulties. Thank you for allowing me to be part of your self-discovery and growth journey.

—W.M.

Dedicated to my five beautiful children . . . I love watching each of you grow and marvel at the human beings you are! I hope you always embrace your strengths AND challenges. Falling down is fine, getting up and facing a new day is even better. And to my wonderful husband Pete . . . you have showed me how to make parenting reflective and joyful. Being a working mom is possible because of you. Much love.

—D.C.

Contents

Reproducible Forms

> **You can download and print these forms at
> freespirit.com/special-ed.**

Introduction

If you are reading this book, you probably get extra help or special education at school, or you have learned that you will. You may have lots of feelings about that. You might also have questions. This book will help you answer those questions.

Some of the following questions might also apply to you:

- Do you sometimes struggle or feel frustrated in school?

- Do you feel nervous about how other kids may react to you because you get special education?

- Do you worry that getting extra help or special education (often called special ed) means you will miss out on other activities?

- Do you wonder whether there is one "right" learning style or whether learning differences affect many students?

- Are you curious about the differences between working with a special education teacher, a classroom teacher, and other adults who might help you?

- Do you want to know more about *why* you sometimes struggle in school and how you can do better?

- Do you wonder about how you can feel good about yourself, even though you have some difficulties in the classroom?

- Do you want to know how to focus on your strengths and your abilities?

If you answered yes to any of these questions, keep reading. **This book is for you!**

How This Book Can Help You

Imagine if a person decided to take a trip without using a map or making any plans. Yikes! Information is very important when people start any kind of experience. This is true for you, too. Whether you're just starting with special education or you've been getting special education help for a while, you're on a journey. It can be helpful for you to learn more about what special education means for **YOU**. You can find out about learning styles, your strengths, your difficulties, and what special help is available for you, now and in the future. You might also want to know more about what kind of help you may need as you go through school, and about the team that will help you. Maybe you want to know how to handle questions from friends. Or you might want to know more about speaking up for yourself so you can get the help that works for you. You will find all of those answers and more in this book.

You are about to read how teachers can support you and what you can do to help yourself. You will find out how you can get help with things that are hard for you. You'll learn about different kinds of help that kids get, and why. You will learn that even really smart kids, who are sometimes called "gifted," might have trouble in some areas of learning, such as math or reading. Needing extra help is not about whether or not you are smart. It's about teaching you in a way that is best for your learning style and it focuses on areas that might be a struggle for you right now.

If you've already been getting help, you will learn more about how teachers know what help is just right for you. You will also find out what you can do to get the most out of this help. For example, you can let your extra help teacher know what you understood in class and what confused you. You can also be part of making some of the decisions that affect you at school.

If you're new to special education, you will get a plan that explains what your goals are and how adults will know when you reach these goals. The adults will help you work on areas that are challenging so that you can gain more skills. If you've been receiving special education for a while, you'll find out how to keep improving with your plan.

Sound good? It gets better. **By reading this book, you have already taken a big step.** You are learning more about how to do your best in school and in life.

And this is just the beginning. You will learn many tools and tips that have helped other kids. These tools can help you, too. This book will teach you how to speak up for yourself. It will help you figure out what to say if your friends ask you questions about your extra help. You will also learn how to feel good about yourself and your abilities—what you do well. Some of the skills you will learn include ways to keep a positive attitude and stay organized. *Every* kid (and adult!) can use these tips to feel proud and happy, and to handle tasks more easily.

This book will also help you with things you might worry about. Some kids worry that if they get extra help, they will miss out on other activities at school. They may worry that they will get more work because they have more teachers. Or they might feel like they don't get to make any decisions for themselves. Other kids believe they will have fewer options in the future because they need extra help in school. As you read this book, you will learn how other kids have handled these concerns.

How to Use This Book

There is no one *right* way to use this book. You can read it straight through from beginning to end. Or you can start with a chapter that interests you. You can look in the Contents or the Index to find specific topics. You might read the book by yourself. Or, you might want a parent* or teacher to read it with you. As you read, you may have comments, ideas, or questions about some of the topics and want to discuss them with an adult you trust. **Do you have a "go-to" person or team of people** you can talk to about all of this? Maybe your team includes your parents, your teachers, or even an older brother or sister. (If you share this book with an adult, let him or her know about the special section just for adults at the end of the book.)

You might also want to make notes about things you find interesting or important. Some readers like to take notes in a notebook or on a computer. Others write down thoughts or reactions on sticky notes and place those in the book. Many students read this book and

*Everyone's family is different. When you see the word *parents* in this book, think of the person or people who take care of you. That might be your mom or dad. It could be stepparents or grandparents. Or, it could be some other adult.

then refer back to it later when they want to review specific information. **Do what works for you!**

As you go through this book, you will see that it has different parts. Some sections are stories about other kids who get special education. We wrote these stories after talking with many kids. We have worked with thousands of students. Lots of them got extra help or special education. Most of them wanted to know why. They also wanted to know if it meant something was wrong with them.

We changed names and some details in these stories. We wanted to protect the privacy of students who shared their feelings with us. But all the stories are based on real life. You can see what other kids in special education have experienced. You will read about what they have learned by speaking up and asking questions. And you can use what they have learned to help you in your own life.

At the end of each chapter is a section called **"Quick and Helpful Hints."** This section is a summary of the big ideas from the chapter. It also looks ahead to what you will find in the next chapter. You can download all these hints together at freespirit.com/special-ed.

Also at the end of every chapter is a form that asks you questions about yourself, your feelings, and how you learn. Try to answer these questions *before* you read that chapter. You can write down your answers in a notebook or type the answers into a computer. You can also photocopy the pages and write on the copies. Or you can download and print out copies at freespirit.com/special-ed. These forms will help you think about your questions, worries, ideas, hopes, and future.

Now, are you ready to learn more about special education and how it can help you? Let's get started!

Wendy L. Moss, Ph.D.
Denise M. Campbell, M.S.

CHAPTER 1

Everything Seems to Be Easier for My Friends

Do you ever compare yourself to other people? Lots of people do this. You may want to see if you have abilities or talents that are different from other kids your age. You may look at other kids to see if they have any behaviors or skills that you want to work on, too. Sometimes comparisons can be helpful. But other times, they can lead to kids focusing only on other people's strengths and only on their own weaknesses or difficulties. Maybe you have felt that other students are smarter than you. Maybe you think they learn more easily than you do or they spend less time studying. Maybe it seems like other kids just have an easier time than you with all kinds of tasks or activities. Many kids worry about these things.

Kids also worry about how good they are at specific skills. They might wish they were better at math, reading, basketball, baking, making friends, or playing the guitar. If you have worries like these, **you are not alone.** Many people doubt themselves or feel bad about themselves sometimes. They may feel like they are not "good enough."

In this chapter, you will read about other kids who struggle with doubts like these. You will learn why people might feel frustrated with their abilities. And you will learn why school can be harder for some students than others. You may even find out some interesting things about yourself and your own feelings.

Before reading the rest of this chapter, turn to page 18 and answer the questions on the form there. You can write your answers in a notebook or type the answers into a computer document. You can also photocopy the pages and write on the copies. Or you can download and print out a copy at freespirit.com/special-ed.

Using What You Know About Yourself

How did you answer the questions on pages 18–20? Do you know when you feel frustrated or upset? Do you know how you usually deal with these feelings? If so, you already know quite a bit about yourself. This is really important.

If you aren't sure how you feel, or why, that's okay, too. You'll be able to think more about this as you go through this book. **Congratulations on starting the journey of getting to know yourself better!**

Once you understand how you feel and how you react, you can decide if your responses help you or hurt you. And you can work on changing how you feel or act. Take a look at Danny's story on the next page. It can help you think about your responses.

Danny is 11 years old. He cares about his grades. He wants to do well in everything he tries. But for a while, he has been having trouble with math. He was getting more and more frustrated after each test. He was feeling bad about himself and his abilities. Danny told his mom later, "I kept getting bad grades. I felt like I was just plain stupid! So I decided there was no point studying my math. I thought my life would be easier if I gave up on school."

Danny thought he'd found a plan that would make things better for him and take away the stress of trying to get good grades in math. But after deciding not to study, he still felt unhappy. One day, after he got another low grade on a math test, he yelled at his mom when she asked what he wanted for dinner. Then he ran to his room and slammed the door. His mom was confused and surprised.

She went to talk with him. Danny was crying. He told his mom about how he had been feeling. It felt good to finally share his secret.

Danny and his mom talked for a long time. Together, they talked about Danny's strengths and difficulties. They agreed that math was a challenge for him, but they also discussed how he had many abilities that he could feel proud of. His mom explained that everyone has weaknesses and strengths, and that it's important to focus on both.

Danny enjoyed focusing on his abilities. In fact, he typed up the list of his strengths and printed it in large, bold type. Then he taped this positive list to his bookcase. Whenever he felt down or upset, he looked at the list and remembered that there was more to him than just his challenges with math. Danny and his mom also came up with a plan to handle the trouble he was having in math.

Here was Danny's plan:

- I will ask my math teacher for extra help.
- I will do my homework with my mom nearby so I can ask for help if I need it.
- I will raise my hand in class to ask questions when I don't understand.
- I will remind myself that no one is perfect. And even though math is hard for me, I'm not "stupid."

After Danny talked with his mom, he saw that the way he had tried handling things wasn't working. Then he was able to find better ways to cope. Have you ever felt like Danny did? Could any parts of his plan help you?

Think about how you react to different situations. For example, if you were playing baseball and you struck out, would you quit playing? Or would you try to figure out how to hit the ball more frequently? Or, suppose that you are really good at geography, but you are also shy. Would you avoid competing in the geography bee because you didn't want to be on stage? Or would you ask others for advice on being confident in front of a crowd? Once you know how you usually react to challenges, you can learn how to deal with difficult situations better. These new ways can help you feel calmer and happier.

Lots of people become uncomfortable or nervous when they don't feel confident. Keeping their insecurities, anxiety, or self-doubts a secret and never asking for help can cause people to feel lonely or sad. But some kids ask for help all the time. They don't believe they can handle any new experiences on their own. It's important to find the right balance for you between getting help when you really need it and also relying on yourself when you can.

To find the right balance, ask yourself these questions, then try using the suggested solutions:

- Do I need help starting the task? If yes, I should ask someone to help me get started.

- Do I know how to start, but I don't think I can do the task well? If yes, I can start the task, then ask for help with the next step.

- Can I do the task, but I'd like some encouragement or reassurance? If yes, I can tell someone my plan and ask for feedback or suggestions.

- Do I know I can do the task well? If yes, I don't need to ask for help. But I may enjoy sharing my accomplishments with others.

When you find the right balance for you, it will be easier to feel pride in taking the healthy risk to get help when you need it. At the same time, you will also feel pride in doing some things independently.

Belief: Everything Is Harder for Me

As you try to figure out your abilities and your areas of difficulty, you may fall into a trap called **false beliefs**.

False beliefs are thoughts you have that may not really be true, but they feel true. For example, do you believe that everyone else understands science better than you? It can feel that way, but you don't really know what everyone else thinks or understands. This is likely a false belief. After all, out of all the students in your grade, some of them probably also struggle with science.

Here are some other false beliefs you might have:

- You believe other kids have an easier time learning or studying than you do.
- You think that other kids are all smarter than you.
- You feel like it's harder for you to make friends, or that all of the other kids are funnier than you.
- You wish you could draw really well or run really fast, and it seems like everyone else can do these things except you.

As you learned at the beginning of this chapter, it is common to compare yourself to other people. And since you spend a lot of time at school, you might do this a lot with people in your classes. Have you ever had some of these common thoughts?

- I study more than other kids, but I still get lower grades.
- Almost everyone in my class feels okay asking questions, but I'm too embarrassed.
- Most kids are a lot smarter than me.
- My teacher likes other kids more than she likes me.
- Other kids were born with lots of talents and abilities, and I didn't get any!
- Other kids remember stuff better than I do.
- Things are just easier for other kids. Everything is harder for me.

Remember, it is normal to think these things sometimes. You may have looked at other kids in class and made some guesses about their skills. But these are just guesses. They most likely are probably not exactly right.

Have you ever heard this saying?

Don't judge a book by its cover.

It means that you can't know what a book is about based only on the title and cover. For instance, what would you think a book called *Old Yeller* is about? Do you think it might be about a person who shouts a lot? That's a pretty good guess. But the book is really about a boy and his dog. A cover or a title of a book might give you clues. But to know for sure what it is about, you have to read the book.

This is also true about your beliefs about other kids. We can make guesses about other people. But we might be totally wrong. It's not easy to know what other people feel or think if they don't say it or show it in their body language. Think about Oscar's story.

Oscar is 12 years old. He gets good grades and he is on the honor roll. His teachers seem to like him and he often answers questions in class. For the last two years, he has also won first place in the science competition.

What guesses might you make about Oscar? Do you think everything is easy for him? Is he smarter than other kids? Is he "perfect"?

If you know someone like Oscar, you might think everything is easy for him. But this may not be true. For exam- ple, Oscar did not always do well in school. He used to

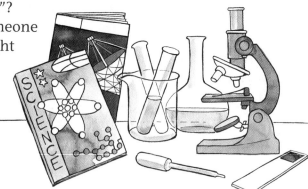

have trouble with some things and he wanted to do better. So he started studying for two hours every night and going in before school once a week for extra help. He also talked with his older sister whenever he was confused about a homework assignment. And he spent time each weekend with his neighbor who was a retired science teacher. Together they did science experiments and talked about what Oscar could do on his own for the science competition.

Most other kids did not know these things about Oscar. They didn't know how much effort and time he spent studying and working to get good grades. What kids show at school may not give you the whole story about how they think, feel, or learn. You need more information to really understand why some kids succeed and others struggle.

This information can help you understand yourself better, too. When you succeed at a project or test, what did you do to make that happen? If you are having trouble with something at school, look closer at that, too. Why do you think you are having trouble? How do you think you could do better? Who could help you come up with a new plan? These are complicated questions. So once you think of someone who can help you work on your plan, see if that person can also help you answer some of these other questions.

Learning More About a Very Important Person—YOU!

Kids struggle in school for many different reasons. You may never know exactly how another kid studies, thinks, or feels. But you *can* know this about yourself. Why is this important? Because when you know how you deal with challenges, you can notice responses that do not work well. Then you can find better ways to handle tough situations.

Take a look at this list of responses that do not usually help solve a problem:

- When I feel frustrated, I get angry or nervous. Sometimes I just give up.

- I try never to admit that I'm struggling and need help.

- I try not to let my friends know that I need help, because I don't want them to make fun of me or not want to hang out with me.

- I tell my teachers and parents "I don't get it" before I even try the work on my own.

- I know I can't do this work anyway, so why try?

- When I know I can do the work, I want it to be perfect. If it isn't perfect, I feel upset.

- I often put off doing work so I can have fun.

- I don't feel like I have any study skills.

Do you use any of these responses when you run into challenges at school? If so, that's okay for now. Learning how you deal with frustration and other tough feelings is important. And even if you don't have the best tools right now for dealing with difficulties, there's good news. This book can guide you toward getting the help you need. And it can show you some positive ways to deal with stressful times and self-doubts. Think about Emily's story.

Emily is 10 years old. She used to use strategies that did not work for her. She didn't ask for help, though. Emily loved going to school because she liked hanging out with her friends. But she did not like studying. Emily told her brother, "When I tried to do my homework I just felt confused and nervous. So I decided I wouldn't do it anymore. At school I acted like I understood stuff, because I wanted my friends to think I was smart. And at home, I just relaxed instead of studying."

What do you think of Emily's way of dealing with her schoolwork? Have you ever used a similar plan? Many students relax or play instead of studying, at least some of the time. Other kids want their work to be perfect and don't ever seem to relax until it is done. But what happens if you use either of these plans every day? If you do not study at all, it will be hard to get high grades. If all you do is study, it will be hard to find time for other activities in your life.

By the middle of the school year, Emily's grades were dropping. Her teacher had talked to her many times about putting more effort into her classwork. And after her parent-teacher conference, Emily's parents were worried and angry that she wasn't working hard. Emily's self-confidence was low because she felt overwhelmed. After months of not asking for help and not doing her work, she was confused about the material. What bothered her most was that her friends had stopped inviting her to study sessions. They did not like how she distracted them with jokes rather than focusing on what they needed to learn and get done.

After reading about Emily, can you see why her strategies did not work well? She needed to find a different solution to her challenge. She finally talked with her parents about what was going on. She told them how hard it was for her to do well in school, even when she studied. After talking with her parents, Emily started getting extra help in school. She began to understand more of the work. And she felt relieved that she didn't have to hide her confusion anymore.

Maybe you feel like Emily. If you have been doing something that is not working for you, you can look for new solutions. Think about friends or classmates who seem successful in school. You could ask them how they handle schoolwork, studying, and stress. If you feel too nervous or shy to talk to your classmates about this, you could talk with teachers about what has worked for other students. And keep reading this book to learn even more ideas about what to do next and what kind of extra help you may need to succeed.

Looking for New Solutions

As you think about what skills are hard for you and how you can do better, remember one important thing: **Everyone has areas that are easier or harder for them.** And to do better in any area—easy *or* difficult—it takes hard work. This is true for the award-winning dancer, the spelling bee champion, and the sports star. They all worked hard to be their best.

Of course, working hard isn't always fun. And it is not easy. You might not like studying very much. You might have trouble paying attention in class. And working hard does not always lead to the results you really want. Sometimes, kids still struggle even when they work hard. They might have a subject or skill that is difficult for them, even though they put in lots of time and effort to do well.

Is this true for you? If so, that doesn't mean that you should insult yourself by calling yourself names like "stupid" or "dumb." That will not help you feel better, do better, or understand more.

What it does mean is that you can look for a new plan. It's okay to admit that you have not yet found the right ways to understand and complete all of your schoolwork. In fact, it is more than okay. It is a smart decision to ask for help and to accept it. Maybe that's why you are reading this book. If you are looking for ways to get help, and to feel comfortable with this support, keep reading! You will learn about how teachers can help you figure out your learning style (how you learn best). You will also find out more about what kind of help might be right for you.

Quick and Helpful Hints

In this chapter, you started on the journey toward understanding yourself. You also read about the pitfalls of comparing yourself to others.

Here are some big ideas to remember from Chapter 1:

- Knowing how you react to difficult situations can help you deal with them better.
- You don't really know how other people study or learn. That's why it's better to focus on yourself, rather than focusing too much on others.
- Everyone needs help sometimes. It's okay to ask for help *and* to accept it. In fact, it's smart!

In Chapter 2, you will think about how you would feel if adults say you need extra help. You can also think about how this help might improve your life. And you will learn ways to *ask* for specific help if you think you need it.

How Well Do You Know Yourself?

You can get to know yourself better by answering the following questions about how you handle frustration and self-doubts. Don't worry about answering the "right" way. Just answer honestly.

1. Do you have worries or doubts about yourself? Do you sometimes feel bad about yourself?   ○ YES   ○ NO

   If you answered yes, who can you talk with about these feelings?

   _____

   _____

2. Do you worry that you seem to have a harder time doing some things than your friends or other kids you see?   ○ YES   ○ NO

3. Do you keep your worries secret?   ○ YES   ○ NO

4. Do you share your worries with someone you trust?   ○ YES   ○ NO

   If you answered yes, who do you usually talk with about your worries?

   _____

   _____

5. Do you feel that you work super hard but still don't do as well as you want to?   ○ YES   ○ NO

6. Do you ever feel sad or angry because
   you think that you are not smart?　　○ YES　○ NO

7. Do you ever worry that you might
   be stupid?　　○ YES　○ NO

8. Do you ever feel super frustrated?　　○ YES　○ NO

9. Can you usually figure out what is
   frustrating you?　　○ YES　○ NO

   If you answered yes, what are some examples of times or
   tasks that often lead to frustration for you?

   _____

   _____

10. Do you ever feel afraid that something
    is wrong with you?　　○ YES　○ NO

    If you answered yes, write down the name of at least one
    person you can talk with about these fears.

    _____

    _____

11. Do you ask for help for everything
    because you do not feel that you can
    handle things on your own?　　○ YES　○ NO

12. Can you name at least one reason why
    you feel really confident and one reason
    why you doubt yourself?   ○ YES   ○ NO

    If you answered yes, use this space to write down one
    reason why you feel confident and one reason why you
    have self-doubts.

    _____

    _____

    _____

13. Do you ask for help sometimes to
    understand work better?   ○ YES   ○ NO

    If you answered no, what stops you from asking
    for help?

    _____

    _____

    _____

14. Do you like figuring out or learning
    some things by yourself?   ○ YES   ○ NO

15. Do you remind yourself that you have
    abilities and talents, even if some things
    are hard for you?   ○ YES   ○ NO

CHAPTER 2

What Extra Help Can Mean for You

Everyone wants or needs extra help at some point. For example, if you aren't feeling well, you may go to your doctor. He or she has special skills for figuring out how to help you feel better. Adults get extra help, too. A grown-up might need help fixing a computer, learning a language, or cooking dinner. It's normal to ask for help when things are hard for us.

If you are reading this book, you probably need some extra help and support at school. You might have a lot of different feelings about that. In this chapter, you will learn why some kids like getting special education help. You also will read about how some kids *don't* like getting it, or even dread it at first. You will learn more about how to understand the help, why you are getting it, and whether you have any control over it. And you'll learn some important ways you can feel *good* about it.

Before reading the rest of this chapter, answer the questions on pages 38–41 and think about your answers.

Why Am I Getting Extra Help?

When it comes to getting special education, you may wonder, "Why me?" Kids get extra help and special education for three main reasons.

Reason #1: One reason you might get extra help is because your teacher has noticed that you are having some trouble in class. He wants to give you more support. Teachers might think about questions like these:

- Do you learn information easily in a large group?
- Do you feel comfortable asking questions?
- Are your test grades showing that you need more help with learning?
- Are you able to focus in class?
- Can you sit still to do the work that you need to do?
- Are you calm enough to be ready to learn?

As you look at this list, you might notice something important. The list does *not* say that your teacher wants you to get extra help because he doesn't like you. It does *not* say it's because he thinks you aren't smart. And it does *not* say it's because he wants to punish you. Teachers want students to get extra help because they want their students to succeed. Maybe your teacher thinks that you can learn better if you have more time to talk about lessons. Or he may think that you will ask more questions in a smaller group.

Reason #2: Another reason you might get extra help is because your parents are worried about how you are doing in school. For example, they may want you to get more support if you are struggling a lot with homework. At parent-teacher conferences, your parents might have learned that it is hard for you to focus in class. Or maybe you aren't doing as well in school as your parents think you can do (or as well as you used to do). Your parents want you to get support to learn as well as you can.

Reason #3: The third reason you might get extra help is because *you* have noticed these things about yourself. Maybe you believe you aren't learning schoolwork as fast or as well as others. You may feel confused or distracted in class. You might be disappointed with your grades. If any of this is true for you, you might feel relieved to learn that help is available.

One or more of these reasons might be true for you. The important thing to remember is that **extra help is meant to help you, not hurt you.** Many students in special education describe it in positive ways. For example, **Gabriel** is 9 years old. He describes special education as "a way for me to learn better."

Knowing What Questions to Ask

You may have lots of questions about your extra help. Your biggest question might be something like, "What does special education mean for me personally, day by day?"

There is no single answer to this question. Special education can be different depending on where you live, what school you go to, and what grade you are in. It can even be different for each student. Your teachers and parents also have a say in what kind of extra help is best for you. (You may have a say, too.)

Still, some forms of extra help are pretty common. The next few pages cover some of these types. As you read about each one, think about questions you might have if you get that type of help. You might want to write down your questions or type them on a computer so you remember them when you have a chance to ask someone about them.

Most teachers set aside time to offer extra help to anyone or everyone in their class. Teachers may offer specific times each week when students can come talk about lessons, ask questions, or get extra help reviewing material. This type of help may be especially popular right before a test.

If your teacher offers this type of help, here are some questions you might want to ask him or her:

- "How do I get this help? Should I just show up?"

- "If I'm not sure when extra help is, how can I find out?"

- "Will I be the only one getting extra help?"

- "I feel embarrassed saying that I need help because I don't want you to think I didn't try. How can I get help but not feel embarrassed?"

- "What if I can't go for help at the time you set up?"

Some kids set up study groups where they give each other extra help. For example, **Olivia** is 10 years old. She easily understands math lessons, but has trouble organizing her writing. Her friend **Ali** is also 10. She loves to write and even enters writing contests. She struggles with math, though. So the two friends set up study sessions together to help each other out. Sometimes students get special education help at school with a teacher. But they can also brainstorm with other students in study groups.

If you are thinking about joining a study group, here are some questions to think about:

- Is this group just an excuse to talk with friends? If so, this might be fun but may not help you understand the work better.

- Are you the main "teacher" in the group? Or is everyone focused on teaching you?

If you answered yes to any of these questions, your study group may not be the right situation for you. It's best if all kids in a group help others, and also get help from others. Your extra help teacher may be able to talk with you about finding a group that's right for you.

A lot of kids get special education from a teacher who goes to classrooms and gives extra help to different kids in different classes all day long. If a special education teacher comes into your classroom to help out, he or she may be called a consultant teacher. This teacher may help all the kids in the classroom but pay special attention to students who need extra help.

Here are a few questions you might have about this kind of help:

- How do I let this teacher know if I am confused?

- Will I have my regular teacher talking to the class and this other teacher talking to me at the same time?

- Would I sit in a separate place in the room during this help or at my regular desk?

- When would I ask the regular teacher a question? When would I save the question for the extra help teacher?

Many students get extra help in a special room with a special education teacher who is an expert at guiding kids in their learning. This room is often called a resource room. Kids who go to a resource room get help in small groups and work on their specific goals.

If you go to a resource room for your help, the work you do will focus on what you need help with. If you struggle with reading, you'll practice reading. If you need support in math, you'll work on math skills. **The resource room is a safe and supportive place.** You can admit what you need help with and ask your questions. You can also learn in a smaller group and get more teacher attention than in your main classroom. At first it might feel strange or scary to leave your usual classroom. It can be frustrating to know you need extra help. But it can also feel great to know that you are getting the right help for you.

If you leave your regular classroom during the day to go to the resource room, here are questions you might have:

- What if I miss some lessons in the classroom because I'm at the resource room?

- Do I get more work than other kids because I have two teachers?

- Will I get different work or different tests?

Your extra help might look like one of the types that you just read about. Or it might combine several types. Your school may even have other creative ways to help students. Some students get extra help for only a short period each day or a few times each week. Some students benefit from longer sessions in the resource room. And other students are in a class with a special education teacher more frequently. It all depends on what you need and the best plan to support you.

After learning what you will do in extra help and how often you will get the help, you may still have questions. Here are some common questions other kids have asked:

- Why do adults think I need to be here?
- How long will I get this help?
- When do I go?
- What will I miss in class?
- Who will be in my group?

You have a right to know what's going on. This is about you and your life, after all! Make a list of your questions and talk about them with your extra help teachers. To get the best answers to your questions, try the following tips:

- Find the right time to ask your questions. This means picking a time when your teacher is not too busy with other students or other work.
- Even if you feel frustrated, do your best to be respectful and polite when you ask your questions.
- Be honest about your feelings, but try to stay calm.
- If you don't understand the answers, keep asking until you *do* understand. You may not like some of the answers, especially if you don't feel like you need or want help. But it's important for you to know and understand why adults have recommended help for you.

How Kids Feel About Getting Extra Help

It's natural to have different feelings about getting special education, whether you just started getting help or have been getting it for a long time. And kids who get the same extra help can have different feelings about it. For example, here's what two students said about their help.

Curtis is 12 years old. One day he came home from school and slammed the front door. He told his dad, "My teacher hates me. She makes me sit with her and do *more* math than other kids. Doesn't she know I hate math?" Curtis felt like his teacher was picking on him by giving him extra help. Curtis was also afraid other kids would think he was "stupid." He wished that instead of getting extra help he could just magically understand his math work. When Curtis did go for his help, he didn't ask any questions. He was so unhappy that he wasn't able to focus on what his teacher said. He just kept thinking about how much longer he had to be there.

Rima is also 12. She feels totally different than Curtis about extra help. Unlike Curtis, Rima was relieved and excited when she started getting extra math help. Before getting this support, Rima used to tell her sister, "I hate math. I feel like such an idiot when I'm in class. It seems like everyone knows the answers but me." After Rima started going to extra help, her whole attitude changed. After a few months, she told her mom, "I'm not an idiot after all! I still don't love math and it's not easy for me. But my extra help teacher explains things slowly. Plus, I get to ask lots of questions. I leave knowing more about math than I ever thought I could."

Did you know that a person's attitude can make extra help easier or harder? Think about Curtis and Rima. Curtis went into extra help feeling negative about it. He just wanted it to be over. Rima went to extra help feeling positive about it. She was eager to learn and understand more. Can you guess which student started doing better in math? Rima started to understand the work and felt more confident. Curtis felt embarrassed and tuned out his extra help teacher. His math work did not improve. And he didn't feel good about it, either. **Having a positive attitude doesn't fix everything. But it DOES make learning easier!**

If you don't feel good about getting extra support, it's okay to admit that. It's important to be honest about your feelings. Then you can work on feeling more positive.

Getting and Keeping a Positive Attitude

When you have a positive attitude, it's easier to learn. But it is not always easy to feel positive or to stay positive. How can you learn to do this? Here are four important tools for getting and keeping a positive attitude.

Positive Attitude Tool #1: Use Positive Self-Talk. "Self-talk" means the things you say to yourself and the way you think about yourself. Do you ever say negative things about yourself? This happens a lot when kids feel stressed or upset. For example, if you get a low grade on a paper, you might tell yourself that you are dumb. This is *negative* self-talk.

How you think makes a difference in how you feel. If you think you are not smart, you are not going to feel smart. But there is good news. You can replace negative self-talk with positive self-talk. Think about Charlie's story.

Charlie is 11 years old. He was nervous about a test coming up. He was afraid he would not do well. Charlie started using negative self-talk. He told himself, "I always get bad grades. I'm never going to learn this stuff."

Charlie's teacher suggested that he talk with the school psychologist. The psychologist helped him learn about positive self-talk and how it could help him. Together, she and Charlie came up with positive self-talk that he can use when he starts to have negative thoughts. Now he says to himself, "I feel good about the fact that I'm trying hard and asking for help when I need it. I also did a good job reviewing my work every night this week. Even if I don't get a high grade, I'm proud of how hard I worked. And if I make mistakes, I know I can review them later with my extra help teacher. This will help me understand the work better."

Using positive self-talk means saying things that a supportive friend would say to remind you that you are special. However, *you* can become that supportive friend and say those positive things to yourself.

Here are some quick tips for using positive self-talk:

- Remind yourself of your abilities.

- Remind yourself that even if you struggle in some areas, wanting to do well is a positive.

- Try these fill-in-the-blank sentences (and fill in the blanks!):

"Even though I have a hard time with _____, I am proud of myself because _____."

"No one is perfect, so I'm just being human if I have some difficulties in _____."

- If you aren't sure what is positive about you or what talents you have, ask trusted adults. Then remind yourself of these abilities often.

Positive Attitude Tool #2: Find Ways to Feel Calm. When you feel calm, you can focus better on learning. But sometimes it is hard to stay calm. Here are some ways you can feel less stressed, even in difficult situations:

- **Deep breathing.** Breathe in slowly through your nose. Imagine you are smelling your favorite food. Next, hold your breath for three seconds. Then, slowly breathe out through your mouth. Imagine you are trying to use your breath to slowly move a feather across a table. Keep doing this for a few minutes until you feel calm and focused. If this doesn't lead to you feeling calmer, try one of the following activities.

- **Exercising.** Get moving! What physical activities do you enjoy? Maybe you like dancing, playing soccer, riding your bike, or playing catch. Maybe you love walking your dog or going for a jog. Whatever you choose, moving your body can help you feel calm and relaxed.

- **Focusing on your body.** You can do this exercise anywhere, even in places you might not expect. For instance, you might be able to do this while waiting in line for something. However, it might be easier if you have some quiet time and you are sitting comfortably. Close your eyes (if you are sitting and in a quiet place). Begin tensing (or tightening) your muscles one by one. Then relax them. Start with your forehead. Tense up your muscles there. Then relax them. Next, tense up your nose so it gets all wrinkled. Now relax your nose. Keep doing this with all your muscles, from your head down to your toes.

- **Using your imagination.** Think of a wonderful, calm memory. For example, remember relaxing at a place you really like. Or, imagine yourself in a calm and beautiful place that you create in your imagination.

- **Using positive self-talk.** Think about what you learned on page 29 about positive self-talk. Choose a few of the nice things you came up with to tell yourself. (Or come up with some now.) You can tell yourself these things whenever you feel upset.

- **Counting.** Try counting slowly from 1 to 10. Or count backward from 10 to 1. You can even count up to or down from 100. Or count by twos or threes if that works for you.

Try these tools and see which ones work best for you. The more you practice them, the easier it will be to use them, even when you feel upset or stressed.

Positive Attitude Tool #3: Talk It Out. It is always okay to ask a trusted adult for support if you are feeling down. This person could be a parent, a teacher, a counselor, or another adult. If you are facing a serious difficulty or if you feel so sad, mad, or nervous that you don't know how to manage or deal with your emotions, seek out an adult who can guide you through your stress. However, if you just need someone to listen to your feelings or about your difficulty, friends or siblings may be good people to turn to as well. Let the person know exactly what you are feeling. Say what kind of help you need and why you need it. Remember to pick a time to talk when the other person has time to really listen. And even if you are unhappy, try to stay respectful as you talk. This will help the other person listen better.

Talking out your thoughts and feelings may come naturally to you, or you might not be sure how to start the conversation. **Here are a few tips on how to begin talking about your feelings and needs:**

- Make sure both you and the other person have time to talk. For example, if you're rushing to catch the school bus, that's not a good time to start the conversation.

- Not all people are comfortable talking about feelings. If the person seems uncomfortable, find someone else who is better able to support you.
- When you begin the conversation, explain the following things:
  - the situation that is making you feel stress
  - any feelings you are having in this situation
  - the ways you have already tried to cope with the difficulty
  - what specific help you need from the other person

Positive Attitude Tool #4: Believe in Yourself. Keep reminding yourself of your talents, abilities, and special qualities. It can help to make a list of your skills, things you do well, and things you like about yourself. Keep this list somewhere handy. Make a few copies if you need to. Then you can look at it whenever you are feeling down. It will help boost your spirits and spark a positive attitude.

Also, remember that focusing on your strengths doesn't mean only when you get a good grade or when you find a school subject easy. It means focusing on *you*! What is special about you? Here are some examples of special qualities that other kids have shared about themselves:

- "My friends can always count on me."
- "I have a real talent for drawing."
- "I take my responsibilities seriously and do my chores."
- "I am kind and patient with my younger sister."

Do you share some of these talents and abilities? Or do you have others that you are proud and happy about? Thinking about these qualities can help you **remember what's great about being you.**

The four positive attitude tools you just read about can help you feel good about yourself, even when you face challenges. For help remembering and using the tools, go to page 42. It is a shorter version of this information that you can photocopy, or you can print a copy online from freespirit.com/special-ed. Keep this page somewhere handy and use it to remind yourself of these tools whenever you like.

Over time, you will find other tools that work for you, too. Don't be afraid to ask your parents or other people who know you well what tips they have for you. Remember, everyone needs help sometimes. You are not alone.

What to Say If Friends Ask Why You Get Extra Help

Sometimes kids feel uncomfortable going to extra help because they don't know what to tell other kids about it. Does this describe you? Knowing how to quickly answer questions can take away some of the stress. You might even be surprised at how well your answers work. Many times, if you answer these questions calmly and casually, other kids will just say "Oh, okay."

Some students like getting help and don't mind if others notice. For example, here's how Ahmed and Stephen handled questions about their extra help.

Ahmed is 12 years old. He meets with his special education teacher every Tuesday and Thursday. When some friends asked why he does this, Ahmed calmly answered, "She helps me with my writing. I hate writing! But she's giving me some tips that make it easier for me. When I'm having trouble writing an essay, I show her where I'm stuck. She helps me figure out a plan for getting unstuck."

Ahmed has a positive attitude about his extra help. He is ready to listen and learn when he arrives. And he feels comfortable telling his friends about it.

Stephen is one of Ahmed's friends. He is 13 years old. Like Ahmed, he has a hard time with writing. But he was embarrassed to ask for help. After he heard Ahmed talking about the extra help like it was no big deal, Stephen felt more comfortable admitting that he needed some extra help with his writing. He asked the teacher if he could get extra help, too. Now Stephen is also learning more easily and feeling more confident about his writing.

Even if you feel good about your help, you might not always know what to say when kids ask about it. Think about using responses like these:

- "I'm going to work on my essay with Ms. Friedman."

- "Just like you have your clarinet lessons, I have reading lessons."

- "I'm getting extra help to figure out the math homework."

When you give your answer, try to make eye contact with the person who asked the question. Stand up straight, or sit up tall. Use a calm, clear voice. If you sound comfortable with getting extra help, most kids won't think it's a big deal. If you hide your special help or seem embarrassed, kids may think it's a big, interesting secret. If you are worried about being teased, remember that if you act calm and confident, other kids may not feel like teasing you. But if someone does tease you, talk with your teachers or parents about how to handle it. You can also read more about dealing with teasing in Chapter 5.

Speaking Up for Yourself

Once you know what extra help you will receive, it's time to think about what you want to get out of the help. Talk about your personal goals with a person who is helping you. Also, the more specific you are about what confuses you with your homework or a class lesson, the easier it will be for others to help you. Don't expect your teacher to be a mind reader! **If you don't share what is difficult for you, other people won't always know.** So, speak up. Of course, it's also important to be respectful. Here's how Frank and Tanya spoke up.

Frank is 9 years old. He wanted to get better at reading aloud so he could read in front of his class. **Tanya** is 10. She wanted help memorizing her multiplication tables. Both Frank and Tanya took the time to think about what they needed help with. Then they spoke up for themselves. They clearly and respectfully shared their needs and goals with their special education teachers. Their goals became part of the focus of their extra help.

You will learn more about speaking up for yourself in Chapter 7. For now, remember that it's not always possible to get everything you want or need. But it is much *less* likely that you'll get what you want or need if you don't speak up.

Quick and Helpful Hints

In this chapter, you learned a lot about why kids get extra help in school and what help is often available to students. You also learned how to speak up for yourself and ask for specific support. You found out some ways to have a positive attitude. And you learned skills for handling questions from other kids about your help.

Here are some important things to remember from Chapter 2:

- Extra help is there to help you, not hurt you.

- You have the power to keep a positive attitude. You can use four useful tools to do this: using positive self-talk, finding ways to feel calm, talking it out, and believing in yourself.

- Being confident about getting extra help shows others you are okay with it. It also helps you learn better.

- Respectfully speaking up for yourself is the best way to let others know what you need, want, feel, and think.

In the next chapter, you will learn how you can get different help if you are not doing as well as you hoped. You will find out about tests you might take to figure out if you need a new plan.

How Does Getting Special Education Affect You?

Answering these questions will get you thinking more about yourself—what you know about, think about, and feel about getting extra help. You may begin to understand how you can share your thoughts and feelings with others. You may also learn ways to accept or even like the support.

1. Do you understand why you are getting special education?　　○ YES　○ NO

2. Do you know how you feel about getting this help?　　○ YES　○ NO

   If you answered yes, what are your main feelings about it?

   _____

   _____

3. Do you mostly feel good about the help you get?　　○ YES　○ NO

   If you answered no, what might help you feel better about it?

   _____

   _____

4. Have you respectfully shared your feelings with your parents, teachers, or other people?　　○ YES　○ NO

If you answered no, why not?

_____

_____

5. Do you have questions about your
   special education or extra help?   ○ YES   ○ NO

   If you answered yes, do you know
   what questions to ask to get the
   answers you need?   ○ YES   ○ NO

   Brainstorm some questions here:

   _____

   _____

   _____

   _____

   _____

   If you aren't sure what to ask, who could you talk to
   about this?

   _____

   _____

6. Have you thought about how to
   answer questions kids might ask
   about your extra help?   ○ YES   ○ NO

If you answered yes, and you have a response that seems like it might work, write it down here so you remember it:

_____

_____

_____

If you answered no, who could you talk to about this?

_____

_____

7. Do you think that how you act and feel when you get extra help might affect how other kids think about your extra help? ○ YES ○ NO

Why or why not?

_____

_____

_____

8. Do you feel like you have any control over how your extra help will work? ○ YES ○ NO

If you answered yes, are you comfortable with how much control you have? ○ YES ○ NO

Also, who else do you think has control over the extra help you get?

_____

_____

If you answered no, can you think of a way to tell teachers or other adults about your feelings? Write a sentence or two that might help you do this:

_____

_____

_____

_____

9. Do you know the goals that you are working on in special education?   ○ YES   ○ NO

If you answered no, how can you find out what your goals are?

_____

_____

10. Do you know how the adults will decide if you reached the goals you are working toward?   ○ YES   ○ NO

Positive Attitude Tools

These four positive attitude tools can help you feel good about yourself, even when you face challenges. Try them out. The more you practice them, the easier using them will get.

Positive Attitude Tool #1: Use Positive Self-Talk

Using positive self-talk means saying things that a supportive friend might say. Now, *you* can become that supportive friend and say those positive things to yourself! Remind yourself of your abilities and of how hard you are working. Remind yourself that you are special because you are *you*.

Positive Attitude Tool #2: Find Ways to Feel Calm

When you feel stressed or upset, try using methods such as deep breathing, exercising, counting, or using your imagination to calm yourself.

Positive Attitude Tool #3: Talk It Out

If you are feeling stressed, sad, or anxious and need help to feel better, ask a trusted adult (like a parent, teacher, or counselor) for support. Or, if you just need someone to listen to what's going on in your life, friends or siblings may be good people to turn to as well.

Positive Attitude Tool #4: Believe in Yourself

Remind yourself of your talents, abilities, and special qualities. Thinking about these qualities can help you remember what's great about being you. Once you figure out what these abilities are, you can use them in your positive self-talk.

CHAPTER 3

Figuring Out How Testing Can Help You

If you are getting extra help in school, you might expect that you'll soon start getting better grades and that it will get easier for you to learn. **Right?** Well, the answer could be: yes, no, or sometimes. For example, maybe you need a little extra time to learn math. Extra help can give you that time. After a while, your math grades might get better. But this may not happen right away. And it could turn out that you need more extra help or a different kind of help that works better for you.

Many kids improve with extra help. But it's important to know that many kids who benefit from extra help might still have a hard time in school. This does not mean these kids will always struggle. It just means that adults need to learn more about why these students are still having trouble. Then the adults can come up with a new plan.

One way teachers and other adults can learn more is by giving students special tests. This chapter will tell you about these tests, and answer questions you might have about them. You will also learn about why you might need to **"teach the teachers,"** and how to teach them. Teachers need your help to understand your challenges and abilities. When they have this information, teachers and other adults can find the best ways to support you.

Before reading more, go to pages 58–59 and think about the statements you see there.

Getting Answers

You, your parents, and your teachers can all work together to figure out why you are having a hard time with some subjects or tasks at school. At times, you may be part of the discussions. Here are some questions you can think about. Your answers may help the adults understand you better.

- How old were you when you started having trouble with some schoolwork?

- What grades and comments do you get on your report card? How do you do on classroom tests?

- Over the years, have teachers talked about what was hard for you? If so, did they also say *why* they thought these things might be hard for you?

- Can you clearly describe what is easy for you in school (and even outside of school)?

- Can you clearly describe what you have the most trouble with?

The sooner you can answer these questions, the sooner you can start getting the right support for you. Look at the last question again: "Can you clearly describe what you have the most trouble with?" This is important. If you can explain your challenges well, you are more likely to get the right help. Here's Jennifer's story.

Jennifer is 8 years old. She told her mom, "My problem is reading. I understand a story if someone reads it to me. But I have a tough time figuring out how to blend the letter sounds together to make words. I can do it, but I'm really, really slow. I think that's why I hate reading. It's so hard, and it takes me forever just to read a few sentences."

Jennifer was able to explain exactly what was hard for her. That explanation gave her mom and her teachers valuable information. They learned that she can understand stories when she hears them. But she struggles when she has to look at the words and sound them out herself. She has trouble staying focused on the story when she tries to read it. And it takes her a long time to read the story, so she gets frustrated. Jennifer's teachers decided to give her some tests looking at the specific issues Jennifer said were hard for her. Jennifer felt relieved. She hoped the test results would enable her teachers to help her more.

Learning Styles

People learn in all kinds of different ways. These different ways are called **learning styles.** Figuring out your learning style can be fun. It can also be useful. If you are having trouble with a certain subject, teachers can see if the way they are teaching matches up with your learning style. This information can be very important in getting you the right help. Here are four of the main learning styles.

The Visual Learner. This person likes to see what she is learning. This person may learn best by watching a movie, looking at pictures, or reading a book. **Vanessa** is 12 years old. She loves looking at pictures of people and places in Spain during her Spanish class. She also likes looking at the words she needs to memorize. Vanessa says, "When my teacher talks in Spanish, sometimes I start to daydream. I need to see the words to make my learning easier."

The Auditory Learner. This person likes to hear what he is learning. An auditory learner may like listening to books on an MP3 player and may learn best by listening to teachers explain information. **Jeffrey** is 10 years old. He explains, "I really like listening to the teacher talk about history. But if she shows us lots of pictures, I get distracted."

The Kinesthetic Learner. This person likes to move around and touch things while learning, and likes doing things for herself. A kinesthetic learner might enjoy getting involved in science experiments or making videos showing what she's learned. **Sasha** is 9 years old. After talking with her dad about her learning style, she spoke with her teacher. Sasha said, "I'm better at learning by doing things. Instead of just reading and writing about Ellis Island, can Solomon and I write a play about it? One of us can be a new immigrant and the other person could work at Ellis Island."

You as a Learner. Some learners remember information best by turning it into a song. Other students like to draw information into fun cartoons or other pictures. **Becky** is 11. She needs silence to remember information. **David** is 8 and learns best when he has someone near him who can talk with him about what he just learned. What is *your* style as a learner and student? Be a detective. Try to figure out what activities help you learn and remember best.

As you think about how you learn best, take a look at the sentences that follow. Next to each sentence is the learning style it reflects. **Which sentences describe you?**

- I like listening to my teacher read a book aloud in class. *(auditory learning)*

- I like to learn by touching and using materials. (For example, I like to handle real coins when I'm learning about money.) *(kinesthetic learning)*

- I love watching movies to learn about information. *(visual learning)*

- I like listening to people talking to each other. *(auditory learning)*

- If I move around or act out information, I learn more easily. *(kinesthetic learning)*

- I like doing video chats with friends instead of just talking on the phone, because it helps me focus on what we're talking about if I can see them. *(visual learning)*

Share your thoughts about these sentences with your teachers and parents. If you're still not sure how you learn best, talk with them about this, too. It's not always easy to figure out your learning style, especially if you learn differently in different situations. But it's important to do some detective work about your learning. If teachers know your learning style, you may be able to do schoolwork in ways that better match your style.

Remember, there are many kinds of learners. Many students have more than one learning style. **No learning style is better than any other style.**

Testing Can Find Answers

As you read about on page 45, Jennifer took special tests that helped her understand herself better. The results also helped her teachers know how to teach in ways that were right for her. Not all kids take these kinds of tests, but many do. These tests help teachers and parents gather important information. This happened for Logan. Read his story on the next page.

Logan is 11 years old. He started getting extra help because he was having trouble with writing. He struggled with organizing his essays, spelling words correctly, and knowing the right grammar to use. A few months later, he was still having a hard time. His teachers wanted him to take some special tests. Logan told his cousin, "I'm really nervous. They are going to do some tests on me. Why do they need to poke and prod into my brain? I mean, I know they aren't really going to open up my head. But I'm still scared. What if they find out something really bad about me?"

If you have to take special tests, you might feel like Logan. Some kids get nervous just hearing the word *test.* But these tests are usually different from what you take in class. Some of them don't even involve reading, writing, or math. The goal of the tests is to figure out what you need help with and how you learn best.

Still, you may have questions about why you are being tested. Logan did. After telling his cousin how he felt, Logan talked with his parents and teacher. He asked them lots of questions. And he learned some great information that helped him feel better. This information might help you, too. Here's what Logan found out:

- You can't fail these tests.

- The test results will not go on your report card.

- The results will help teachers understand how you learn best (your learning style).

- The results can reveal specific areas you need help in.

- The test results can also show what you are really good at.

Now, think about what Maggie, Peter, and Evan learned from their tests.

Maggie is 10 years old. After taking special tests, she learned that she has a really good memory for things she sees. It is harder for her to remember things she hears. **Peter** is 9 years old. The tests showed that he knows a lot of different words. However, he struggles to understand math. **Evan** is 12 years old. He learned that he has a hard time following a lot of steps to do a task. He feels confused about what to do first, what to do second, and so on. Evan learned that this is why he has trouble organizing paragraphs in essays. He also gets confused sometimes about the order of the steps he needs to do when working on a math problem. Evan was happy to learn from the tests that he is creative and that he's good at reading.

Maggie, Peter, and Evan learned important information about themselves. Their teachers learned a lot, too. They learned about these students' strengths and weaknesses, and about how to teach in ways that might be better for these students. Everyone's brain works differently. We all have our own ways of learning and thinking about new ideas. Testing can be a great way to learn more about your brain.

Types of Tests

Different schools have different ways of giving tests. Maybe one person will give you one test or several tests. Or multiple people may give you tests. If you want to know who will test you, you can ask your teacher or parents.

In this section, you will read about some common tests and who usually gives them to students. You probably won't take every type of test. If you are tested, adults will choose the tests that will help them better understand your needs and abilities. If you find out that you will take one or more of these tests, you can ask questions first. Talk to the person giving you the tests. (This person is sometimes called an evaluator.) Ask what the test will measure, how long it will take, and if you will get the results. The testers are there to help you. They will probably answer your questions so you feel more comfortable about taking the tests.

Here are some people you might meet and tests they often give to students:

- **School psychologist.** This person is trained to understand how people feel, how they think, and how they learn. He or she can help kids talk about their feelings and deal with challenges. The school psychologist wants to understand your learning style, your abilities, and your challenges when you learn new information. If you meet with this person, you might look at pictures, define words, or even play a game or do a puzzle with blocks. This expert may also ask about *you*. He or she might want to know how you feel about yourself, school, and friendships. You might answer questions about what you think your strengths and your difficulties are.

- **Learning specialist.** This person might also be called an educational evaluator. He or she is an expert at recognizing the skills a student needs to do well in subjects such as reading, writing, and math. This specialist usually gives quick tests that focus on basic abilities that are used in these subjects. You do not need to study for these tests. These tests help identify the kinds of work that are easier for you and areas where you need more help.

- **Speech and language therapist.** This person may also be called a speech and language pathologist. His or her job is to focus on your listening and talking skills.

This person might give you tests to find out how easy or hard it is for you to listen to and understand the teacher when she is talking in class. Other tests might measure how well you are able to share all the information you have in your head. This person can test how clearly you speak or how you organize your thoughts in writing. The speech and language therapist may ask you to listen to a story and then retell it. This expert may also check your ability to follow multiple steps after hearing them, or other skills related to listening and speaking. You don't need to study for these tests, either.

These are just a few of the people who help kids. Other specialists are experts on vision, coordination, handwriting, and much more. Remember, you may not meet with every type of specialist. Instead, you will work with the ones who are right for you. Together they will work on answering one important question: "What help do you need to learn better and feel better at school?"

Think about Matthew's experience.

Matthew is 10 years old. He had a difficult time in school. He told his grandmother, "My handwriting is messy, even when I try my best. I also have trouble with reading. And it's hard for me to line up numbers to do division in math." Matthew met with the school psychologist and with the learning specialist. They both asked him questions and gave him tests. They worked to figure out his learning style, his strengths, and his challenges.

Matthew also met with an occupational therapist. Occupational therapists help people build up physical and visual skills that help them do activities in their daily lives. These experts might work on a person's posture, eye movements while he or she is reading, and other skills.

The occupational therapist studied Matthew's handwriting and how he held his pencil. She also looked at his visual tracking. Visual tracking is the ability to move one's eyes smoothly while reading and to focus on one word at a time, in order, without reading the wrong line or skipping lines. The occupational therapist also looked at how Matthew wrote down numbers when he did math problems. Matthew went to an eye doctor, too, who checked to see if he needed glasses.

Matthew learned a lot about himself from meeting with the occupational therapist and the eye doctor. He learned that his vision was better for seeing far away than for seeing close up. So he started wearing glasses to help him when reading or writing. Also, Matthew learned that his eyes sometimes don't work well together, which makes it harder for him to track words on a page. Most important of all, Matthew learned that people could help him overcome his challenges and do better. He was happy about that.

Common Fears

If you find out that you will take special tests, you may feel relieved. You might be excited to know how you learn best. Many kids feel this way. But it is also common for kids to be worried or scared about what the testing means and what the results may reveal. Here are some common fears kids have about testing.

Common Fear #1: "If I mess up on the tests, the teachers will think that I'm stupid." The people testing you are *not* trying to find out if you are stupid. They expect you to make mistakes on some of the test questions. They do not expect you to be perfect. No one is perfect. We all make mistakes. The tests are meant to help the specialists figure out what *kinds* of mistakes you make and why. This information helps them learn how to help you. And they are not *only* looking for your mistakes. The specialists want to learn about your strengths and what you are really good at, too.

Common Fear #2: "The tests results are going to say I should repeat a grade." Repeating a grade (or being "held back") is a big decision. How you do on your special tests does not determine if you get held back. That's a decision that teachers and parents make after considering a lot more information. The goal of testing is to figure out how you can handle your challenges and learn in a way that works for your learning style. That's it—but that's powerful. Testing is supposed to help you get the right help.

Common Fear #3: "The teachers think something is really wrong with me." It is true that if your teachers think something is keeping you from learning, they might use tests to find out how to help you. For example, **Joseph** is 12 years old. Testing revealed that Joseph gets distracted during spelling lessons because he's bored. **Pauline** is 14. Her teacher learned from the tests that Pauline knows a lot of information but has trouble explaining it when she gets called on. This does not mean something is wrong with either Joseph or Pauline. It just means that changing how they're being taught could help them learn better.

Sometimes, tests will show that a student has a challenge that stops him or her from learning easily. This information can lead to ideas for helping a student. But testing is never about criticizing you. It is not designed to hurt your feelings or make it seem like something is wrong with you. Testing is about discovering your strengths *and* your difficulties. Its goal is to find out how you can do your best.

Common Fear #4: "My teachers and parents are making me take tests because they think I'm lazy. They think that I'll shape up if they scare me with testing." Testing should *never* be a punishment. It isn't meant to scare you. And testing should never be used as a way of motivating you to do better. Testing is meant to help you and your teachers. For example, testing may show that you aren't using all your skills in class. Does this mean that you should be punished? No! It means that it's time to brainstorm new ways to help you use your skills and abilities. For example, **Aidan** is 12 years old. He has been having a hard time staying focused in Spanish class. His teacher offered him a deal. She knew that Aiden loved photographing animals. She told Aidan that if he participated more in class, one of his squirrel pictures could be published in the school newspaper. Aidan really tried to pay more attention in class.

Your Test Results

You might feel a little nervous, excited, or confused about getting the results of your testing. This was true for Jamal.

Jamal is 11 years old. He did not want to know his test results. He was worried that they would be all bad. He told his dad, "Those tests are just going to show that

I'm not smart and that I can't read. They'll say I'm a bad artist. And I know I'll never understand geometry."

After Jamal took his tests, his dad met with some of the teachers who did the testing. Jamal's dad learned a lot about how his son learned. He was happy to know that the people at school saw Jamal's talents and abilities. And he was glad that they had a good plan for helping Jamal.

Jamal's dad thought Jamal would feel better if he learned about his test results. So Jamal and his dad met with one of the people who tested Jamal. They talked about what the tests showed. Before he went to this meeting, Jamal wrote down all the questions he had. He also wrote about how he hoped his teachers could help him. At the meeting, the tester explained Jamal's test results. Then Jamal had a chance to ask his questions.

At the end of the meeting, the tester asked Jamal to describe what he had learned. Jamal said, "I learned that I'm actually pretty smart in a lot of ways. I have two challenges. One is a visual-perceptual problem. The other one is a visual-motor problem. Both of these problems have to do with how I see. They make it harder for me to do reading, art, and geometry. But my teachers have ideas to help me! I feel good about that. I also learned that even super smart people have trouble with some things."

After the meeting, Jamal understood what was causing him stress in school. He had always known he wasn't being lazy. The testing proved that he was right. The tester said that sometimes kids try the same plan over and over again to understand the work. When they still have trouble, they feel frustrated. They need a *new* plan.

Testing is an important way to figure out a new plan. So if you feel nervous like Jamal did, remember that testing can be a good thing. The results may help your teachers design a plan that is just right for you. It will help you use your areas of strength. It may also help you improve at the things that are hard for you.

What Your Test Results Can Tell You

Testing can tell you about much more than your skills in reading, writing, and math. It may reveal how well you understand the words that people say to you. It can tell you how well you share your thoughts when you talk or write. It can help you discover your learning style and how you handle challenges. To get the most out of your tests, talk about the results with your parents, teachers, or testers. Try to get answers to these questions:

- What did you learn about me from the tests?
- What are my areas of talent? What are my strengths? What am I good at?
- What are my main areas of difficulty? What do I often have trouble with?
- Why do I have trouble in some areas?
- What is my learning style?
- How can my teachers help me learn better?
- What goals do I need to work on?

Testing and classwork can be stressful sometimes. You might worry about making mistakes. But remember, it's okay that you are not perfect. **No one is perfect in every way, every day.** Knowing and remembering this can help you relax a little when you have a hard time. It's good to ask for help when you are confused. It's also good to feel proud of your strengths and proud that you are trying to find ways to build up your areas of difficulty.

Quick and Helpful Hints

In this chapter, you learned that people have many different learning styles. You found out why some kids take special tests and what those tests can show. You read that it's very common to be nervous about these tests. But you also learned that these tests can be very helpful. Testing helps you "teach the teachers" about your learning style, your abilities, and why you might struggle with some work.

Here are some of this chapter's important ideas:

- It's okay to make mistakes. No one is perfect!
- Everyone learns a little differently. No learning style is the best.
- Testing is not meant to hurt you. Its goal is to help you. That is why adults who care about you have recommended it.
- Testing can help you and your teachers know more about you and how you learn best.

In the next chapter, you will read more about how your test results can lead to the best support for you and the right team of experts to guide you. You will also get information about the many kinds of extra help available. You may be impressed and happy to know how much help is out there for you and other students.

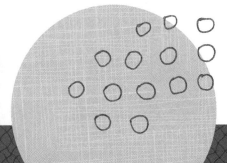

Why Do Students Need to "Teach the Teachers"?

Take a look at the following sentences. They are about why kids getting extra help might need to take tests to find out more about how they learn. They also describe some thoughts or ideas people might have about why kids might need to "teach the teachers." Think about these statements and say whether you think they are *true* or *false*.

1. Teachers and parents want to find out why some work is hard for me.   ◯ TRUE   ◯ FALSE

2. I'm afraid that my teachers and parents think I am stupid.   ◯ TRUE   ◯ FALSE

3. I feel comfortable asking questions about why I'm getting certain tests so I understand what's happening.   ◯ TRUE   ◯ FALSE

4. I have questions about testing and know someone I can ask to help me understand what's happening.   ◯ TRUE   ◯ FALSE

If you answered true, write down the questions and the person (or people) you can ask:

_____

_____

_____

_____

5. Adults think I don't care about my schoolwork. They think that giving me tests will scare me into taking work more seriously.   ○ TRUE   ○ FALSE

6. The adults are trying to figure out what my talents and abilities are. Then they can help me build on these strengths.   ○ TRUE   ○ FALSE

7. My teachers just don't like me. They want to move me into another classroom so they don't have to see me as much.   ○ TRUE   ○ FALSE

8. The information from testing will help teachers teach me in a way that helps me learn.   ○ TRUE   ○ FALSE

9. Testing is going to be hard, boring, and confusing.   ○ TRUE   ○ FALSE

10. My teachers already know what's hard for me, so testing is a waste of time.   ○ TRUE   ○ FALSE

11. If other kids see me in a testing room, they will wonder what's wrong with me.   ○ TRUE   ○ FALSE

CHAPTER 4

You and
Your Team

Congratulations! If you have taken some of the special tests you learned about in Chapter 3, you and your teachers have a lot of new information. You have probably taught the grownups a lot about your abilities and needs. Did you learn some things about yourself, too?

In this chapter, you will get a chance to think more about your strengths, challenges, and learning style. You will learn more about the plan your teachers and parents have made to help you. Your plan will include teaching you in ways that match your learning style. It will help you with things that are hard and also build on your talents.

Fortunately, you won't be doing this alone. **You are a member of a team.** Teachers are part of this team. So are your parents. You might have other people on your team, too. They could include doctors or other experts. You'll read more about your team members later in the chapter.

But first, go to pages 78–79 and read the sentences on the form there. Think about what questions or feelings you may have about your team.

Telling Your Team About Your Abilities and Challenges

You probably already know a lot about what you do well, what you like, and what is hard for you. You may know how to help yourself handle challenges. And testing may have given you even more information about how you learn.

You can teach your team even more about all of these things. As you think about how to share your strengths and challenges, try making a chart. List things that you are good at and things that are hard for you. That's what Nicki did.

Nicki is 10 years old. She loves writing. She also knows that thinking about her strengths and challenges can be useful. She listed these ideas in a chart. Here is what her chart looked like:

Nicki's Strengths and Challenges

STRENGTHS	CHALLENGES
Basketball	Running fast
Softball	Cleaning my room
Being a good friend	Long writing assignments
Cooking spaghetti with Aunt Marie	Organizing my work and papers
Writing short stories	Spelling
Writing neatly	Listening in class
Math	Remembering when tests are scheduled

From her testing results, Nicki learned why listening in class is one of her challenges. She found out that she is a visual learner. She can focus well when she has pictures or diagrams to look at. But when she listens to a teacher talking, it can be hard for her to stay focused. She also learned that she needs help organizing her writing.

Nicki was happy to learn these things about herself. She told her parents, "I'm not lazy! The tests showed I can do math quickly. It's easy for me. They also showed me why I have a hard time in school sometimes. My teacher says now he'll be able to help me better, and I'll learn more."

After Nicki finished her list of strengths and challenges she shared it with her teacher. He said, "Nicki, this is so helpful. I think that writing about sports, cooking, and friendships may be a way for you to be more interested in longer writing assignments. Want to try doing your next writing assignment on the different ways to be a good friend?" He also said that he didn't realize that Nicki struggled to remember when tests were scheduled. He promised to try to help her in this area. Nicki felt proud that she helped her teacher pick assignments that were better for her, and that he would help her remember test dates. She truly felt that she was part of her team now.

Take some time to fill out your own chart. (You can write your chart on notebook paper, type it on a computer, photocopy the chart on page 80, or download and print it at freespirit.com/special-ed.) Make sure to list lots of your talents and abilities. It's good to add things that make you feel happy and things that you often succeed at. But don't forget to add areas that are hard for you. That way, you know what help you might need. There is no right or wrong way to fill out your chart. The important thing is to be honest.

Once you complete your chart, review it. Make sure you described yourself accurately. You may want to ask your parents or other people you trust to look at it, too. They may have additional strengths or challenges for you to add if you want. Then, share your list with your team. **The more your team knows about what comes easily to you and what you need support with, the better able they are to give you that support.**

Who Is on Your Team?

Your team has one big goal. They want you to get the help that is just right for you. They can make this happen in lots of ways. Many different people might work together to support you and other kids.

Who is on your team? Every student has a team that is picked just for them. So, your team may be a little different from the team that another student has. Yours will probably include your classroom teacher. Your parents or other family members may be on your team, too.

Other adults might also be on your team. They may have special skills or knowledge to help you. Check out some of the many people who could be part of your team.

Special education teachers. Your classroom teacher has spent lots of time learning how to teach subjects such as reading, writing, and math to a big group of students. Other teachers, called special education teachers, also know how to teach these subjects. But they usually work with smaller groups of kids. And they have special skills. Special education teachers are trained to work with students who may struggle with learning. They are experts at matching teaching styles to kids' learning styles and needs. If you took special tests, the special education teachers looked at the results to see how *you* learn. Based on these results, special education teachers might recommend that you sometimes learn in a small group. Maybe they will review lessons with you again after you have been taught these lessons in your class. Or they might teach you special tips and tools that will help you learn better.

Counselors. Counseling is a type of help that is a lot like coaching. If you meet with a counselor, that person might be the school guidance counselor. Or it could be a school psychologist or school social worker. This person may teach you problem-solving tools and coach you on how to handle schoolwork challenges. He or she might also talk with you about your feelings and how you handle social situations. You can set up times to talk with a counselor if you feel upset, anxious, or overwhelmed.

Speech and language therapists. The term *therapy* can be confusing. But it really just means a type of help. A speech and language therapist can help you with how clearly you speak and how you understand language. He or she can also help you use language to speak or write more clearly.

Occupational therapists. Occupational therapy is also called OT. Occupational therapists often work on fine motor skills. Fine motor skills are how you use your fingers and hands. OT can also help kids improve their visual-motor skills. Visual-motor skills are how your eyes, hands, and brain work together. For example, **Ramon** is 9 years old. He went to OT because his handwriting was hard to read. He had trouble forming letters. And sometimes his hand would hurt after he wrote a lot. Ramon's occupational therapist taught him exercises to build hand strength. He also gave Ramon fun activities that helped him work on his writing skills.

Physical therapists. Physical therapy is also called PT. Physical therapists help kids with their gross motor skills. Gross motor skills help you when you move around and also help you build strength in your arms and legs.

Bianca is 11 years old. She has cerebral palsy. She uses crutches to help her with balance. Bianca's PT helps her work on her coordination and control of her muscles. These skills allow Bianca to get around more safely and quickly.

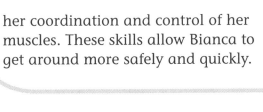

Consultant teachers. A consultant teacher is kind of like a resource room teacher. This person is trained to help students learn in ways that are right for them. The consultant teacher might meet with students to help with specific skills. But usually a consultant teacher spends less time with students than resource room teachers do. The consultant teacher may talk more with the classroom teachers than with students. This expert may try to make changes in your classroom or in your assignments to help you learn better. In other words, this person helps you and helps your teacher set up the right situation for you to learn most easily.

Other experts. Some kids might work with other adult experts who aren't listed here. These might include people who study how kids see or hear. They might also include people with titles like behavioral consultants or technology specialists. You probably won't get every possible kind of help or meet with every kind of specialist.

If you find out that you will work with a person and you don't understand why, ask questions. You can talk to your classroom teacher, a special ed teacher, a counselor, or your parents. **You deserve to understand what help you will get and why.**

Making a Plan

Now you know a bit more about some of the people who may be on your team at school. **One of your team's biggest jobs is to make a plan for you and your learning.**

This plan might be called by a few different names. That's partly because your *team* may have a few different names. For example, you might have a 504 team and a 504 plan. Or you might have a Committee on Special Education and an Individualized Education Program. (You'll read more about these very soon.) Do you feel a bit confused by this? If so, you're not alone. A lot of students and parents are confused when they first learn about the names of teams and plans.

Here's the main thing you need to know: You have one BIG team. It includes everyone who helps you. Sometimes this big team all meets together. But it can be hard to always find time for the big team to meet together. And sometimes the whole team doesn't need to talk. It may only be necessary to get a few people together because the question, problem, or change of plan only involves these people. It's like a baseball coach who wants to help the pitchers work on certain pitching skills. The whole baseball team doesn't need to be there. Only the pitchers go to this special practice session.

Sometimes kids have a type of team called a **Committee on Special Education.** It's also called a **CSE.** This group meets at least once a year. Your school team members are there and parents are usually there as well. One person runs the meeting. He or she is often called the chairperson. You can ask your team if you should attend the yearly meeting and, if so, what you should expect to hear. You can even ask if you should speak about anything and if you can ask questions (if you have any). At this meeting, team members talk about how you have been doing during the school year. They also talk about your goals and the type of help you should receive for the next year. They write a special plan just for you. The plan is called an **Individualized Education Program** or **IEP.** Your team writes this plan to focus specifically on *your* learning, so it is individualized for *you*. That's what the name means.

Or you might have a team called a **504 team.** It is a lot like a CSE. A 504 team may also meet once a year or more to review how things are going for you. And this type of team also makes a plan to help you learn. It is called a **504 plan** (because the 504 team makes the plan). Similar to the CSE meeting, the adults who go to the 504 meeting can include those who work with you in school, your parents, and other people who take care of you. For example, a physical therapist or a medical doctor might write a report for the team if you have medical issues that affect you in school. You can ask your team if you should attend the 504 team meeting, what you might hear if you go, and what role you should have at the meeting.

If you need some special help at school, you might have a CSE team or a 504 team. Remember, these teams are a lot alike. And you won't have both. The adults will decide which team is better able to support you. Whether you have an IEP, a 504 plan, or some other type of plan, it will probably include a few important pieces of information. Here are some of the things that your plan may include:

- how you are doing now
- what goals you will work toward
- how teachers, parents, and you will know if you reach your goals
- information on whether you will have changes in your work responsibilities, how the work is presented, and who might support you in completing work
- how you will be tested on information that you learned
- where you take tests, whether you get tests that are designed especially for you, and whether you get support during testing, such as more time or breaks (not the answers, obviously!)

- what kind of help you will get
- how much extra support you will get each week

Did you know that there are legal reasons why certain plans need to be followed? A law called IDEA was created so that students across the United States could get an appropriate education based on their needs. (IDEA stands for the Individuals with Disabilities Education Act.) This law doesn't mean that kids who get special education necessarily have serious problems or that they can't succeed. It just means that their teachers and schools have a responsibility to help them learn in ways that are right for them.

Parts of the Plan

No matter what kind of team you have or what your plan is called, **your plan will be designed especially for you.** Just like every kid's team may be different, every student's plan can be different, too. Yours might include a few kinds of special help and special support teachers. Here are some examples of the kinds of help you may receive as part of your plan.

Tips and tools. Your teachers may give you some tips and ideas that make it easier for you to learn in class.

Quinn is 12 years old. His teacher suggested that he try using a graphic organizer when he wrote essays. Graphic organizers often use boxes or circles on a piece of paper to help you organize your information before you start writing a paper or essay. Quinn used an organizer with a circle in the middle. That's where Quinn wrote down his main topic, frogs. A bunch of lines came out of the middle circle. Each line had another circle at the end. In those outer circles, Quinn wrote down more information that he wanted to put in his paper, like different kinds of frogs, what frogs eat, and where they live. This tool helped Quinn organize his thoughts and ideas before he started writing.

Kenneth is 14 years old. He also uses a simple tool to help him at school. Kenneth switched from using a notebook for each subject to using one big notebook with four sections, one section for each of his four main school subjects (math, social studies, writing, and science). Before he made the switch, sometimes Kenneth would write in the wrong notebook. For instance, one day, he wrote social studies notes in his science notebook. Then he got mixed up about his homework for those two subjects. Using just one notebook with tabs for each subject has helped him a lot.

Abigail is 11 years old. She has started using the computer to type her essays because she struggles to write neatly and sometimes has a hard time reading her own writing. But she quickly learned to type. Typing her essays on the computer makes it easier for her to read what she has written. That makes it easier for her to revise her essays. Now Abigail feels proud of her essays. She still works on her handwriting, but it doesn't slow her down anymore during writing time.

You may be surprised at how many simple tips and tools are available to help kids.

Classroom and homework changes. As part of your plan, your team might decide to change how you work when you are in the classroom. They might also change how you do your homework. Or, if your teacher offers extra help before school, during a period during the day, or after school, going in for this help might be right for you. Even small changes can be a big help. Here are some changes that teachers made for Maya, Anthony, Becca, and Harold.

Maya is 13 years old. Math is really hard for her. So her team decided she would do just a few problems for homework each night instead of a whole page. That way, she can work super hard on solving and understanding those problems rather than spending the whole night struggling.

Anthony is 10 years old. He has trouble paying attention in class. So his teacher created a special place for him in the classroom where he can do his work with fewer distractions.

Becca is 9 years old. She has a hard time copying from the board. Her teacher started giving her printed copies of the material. Now Becca can focus on listening during class and study the printout later.

Harold is 12 years old. He feels nervous asking questions during class. So Harold's teacher gave him something called a behavior modification plan. (It can also be called a b-mod plan.) With the plan, Harold earns points each time he raises his hand and speaks in class.

In his very first week trying the new plan, Harold earned enough points to get extra computer time. He loves it!

Testing changes. Testing is supposed to measure what you learn and know. You might learn differently from other students. Or some ways of sharing what you have learned may be easier for you than other ways. So you may need a different kind of test to show what you know. Your teacher may be able to change the way your test looks, or give you other help. Here are two examples.

Matthew is 10 years old. You read about him in Chapter 3. He has problems with visual tracking. So his tests have bigger print on them. They also have fewer questions on each page and more space between each question.

Gloria is 11 years old. Her special testing showed that she could do well on classroom tests, but it took her longer than other students to finish them. So Gloria's teacher gave her extra time on tests. This change really helped her focus on doing well without rushing.

Other kids may go into quieter rooms to take tests. Some kids have a grownup read the tests to them out loud. There are many options. If you have trouble with classroom tests, talk to your teacher about what changes might help you. Or share what has worked for you when you took other tests.

Resource room help. As you read earlier, special education teachers often work with small groups of kids in a resource room. This room is separate from the main classroom. Here, special education teachers can give each student more attention. If you go to a resource room, you may work on many skills, including reading, writing, and math. A special education teacher might give you extra explanations of what you learned in your main classroom. She may teach in a way that is a better match for your learning style. It's important to know and remember that kids do not go to resource rooms because they can't learn. They go to get the specific type of help they need to learn *better* and do their best. Many kids do better when they get this extra support.

Joining Your Team Meetings

Your team members will get together during the year to talk. They will talk about your progress and what you might still need help with. Then they will talk about your plan. Maybe it will stay the same. Or maybe it needs to change so that it works even better.

Everyone on your team is important. But **remember that no one on the team is more important than you.** So at some point, you may want to ask if you can join some of your team meetings. That's what Luigi did.

Luigi is 11 years old. He has been getting help from a speech therapist since third grade. He also goes to the resource room for help. But he never knew that his team had a special meeting to talk about him and his goals. When he first found out about this, he was upset. He asked his dad, "Why are they talking about me behind my back? That doesn't seem fair. They don't know what I want to learn. They don't know what's easy or hard for me."

Luigi's dad shared these feelings with Luigi's resource room teacher. Later, Luigi's dad told him, "I learned something important today. You are part of the team. You can even come to part of your meetings if you want. But you need to plan ahead." Like many students who attend their own meetings, Luigi needed to be comfortable listening to what other people said about him and not interrupt or argue. He also needed to know that he could speak up at certain times in his meeting. Luigi's dad helped him write about his own strengths and also his continued challenges. Luigi took what he wrote to the meeting. He knew he could read it, or he could give it to his team. And if he had questions or disagreed with some of the recommendations from team members, he knew that he could ask questions at the meeting or later.

Going to a team meeting can be interesting. It can teach you a lot. But it may be a little scary the first time. It might help to know that if you go to your meeting, you will know a lot of the people there. Your classroom teacher and other team members who work with you in school will probably be there. So will your parent or parents. You might also meet someone called a chairperson. (Some teams include this person and some do not.)

Adults may use some words you don't know at your team meetings. You might hear them talking about your CSE, 504 plan, IEP, or other terms. Remember reading about these terms earlier in this chapter? Adults on your team may also use unfamiliar words to talk about your strengths, weaknesses, and learning styles. If you join a team meeting and are confused about what these words mean, **speak up.** During the meeting, you can politely ask for a short explanation. Or you can talk to one of the adults you trust after the meeting is over.

If you go to your meeting, you will probably hear about:

- how teachers feel you are doing with your work this year
- how comfortable you seem learning new skills
- what might still be tough for you
- what your strengths are

- how you learn best

- what goals they think you can work on in the future

- what plan would be best for you as you continue to learn in school

If you do go to the meeting, you can just listen. But to make the most of the meeting, you may want to spend a few minutes sharing how *you* feel school is going. After all, you're the reason everyone is meeting. You could say what you like about your extra help and what you think could be better. You could also share how you feel you have improved and what help you still want. Here's what Ava did.

Ava is 13 years old. She joined her meeting for only five minutes. She didn't want to listen to the adults talking. She didn't want to sit in a meeting for a long time. She just wanted to know what goals her team planned to set for her. She listened and then thanked them for all the help they gave her. She left and felt good about going to her meeting and sharing her thoughts.

What about you? You don't *have* to go to your meeting or stay for the whole time. Or, you may want to go for as much of the meeting as you can. Sometimes a team sets aside a special time for the student to attend. After that, the student returns to class. You may want to be very involved in the meeting, or you may just want to listen. If you want to learn about the role you might have at the meeting, who can you talk to about this? Try talking to members of your team. They have probably been to lots of meetings and can guide you on how you can get involved.

If you go to your meeting, even for a few minutes, remember a few guidelines that are recommended for all of the people who attend:

- Be respectful.
- Only one person talks at a time. Let someone else finish before you speak up.
- It's okay to ask questions.
- It's okay to share your opinions.
- Stay sitting down (unless you can't for a physical reason).

The meeting will go most smoothly and be most helpful if everyone follows these rules.

Your Role on the Team

There is no one right way to prepare for your team meeting. **Jack** is 12 years old. He likes using computers. So he used his computer to make a presentation for his team. It showed his interests and his abilities. It also showed what he wanted more help with. **Mackenzie** is 8 years old. Before her meeting, she filled out a chart that her resource room teacher gave her. It showed what she liked about the year and what she *didn't* like about how things had gone. Her chart also showed what she was worried about for the next year. **Rochelle** is 10 years old. She loves chatting with adults in her life. She felt comfortable coming to the meeting and talking for a few minutes about her strengths, needs, and goals.

Your role on the team is not to make the adults do exactly what you want them to do. You are definitely a special member of the team. What you think is very important. But **everyone on your team has a special role.** And everyone is working to help you. So even if you share what you want, the adults may not always agree with you. You *could* yell, stomp your feet, or cry. But that probably is not the best plan, right? Here's Malcolm's story on the next page.

Malcolm is 13 years old. He said, "I was so mad during my meeting. I told the adults I wanted to stop going to the resource room. But they said I still needed to go. I wanted to scream and tell them to butt out of my life. My mom gave me one of her looks to remind me to stay cool. So I calmed down and listened. My teachers said why they wanted me to keep going to the resource room. They also listened to my feelings. Mr. Silver said, 'Malcolm, I hear that you want to be doing the same work as your friends and that you want to be in the regular classroom all the time. It sounds like you want to succeed. Resource room isn't going to be recommended if you don't need it, but can you see how math is still hard for you? We want to help you succeed.' I thought for a minute, and then agreed that I still need the help. I liked that Mr. Silver listened to me. I was also glad to know that I won't keep going to resource room if I don't need it."

Remember, everyone on your team and at your meeting is there to help you. They are not there to judge you. And they are not trying to make your life harder. They want to support you and make sure you can succeed.

Quick and Helpful Hints

In this chapter, you learned that you have a team that helps you learn in the best way for you. Lots of people may be on this team. One of their important jobs is to create a plan for supporting you at school. You can help your team make this plan. You may even decide to ask if you can join your team at some meetings.

Here are big ideas to think about from this chapter:

- Special education is about getting the right support for you. You don't have to figure this out by yourself. You have a team to help support you and build up your skills.

- No one plan is right for all students who get special education. Every student has his or her own plan.

- You are an important part of your team, and your voice matters.

In the next chapter, you will get to see what happens once your plan starts. You will find out when your support will begin and what your schedule might look like. You'll also read about how you can handle potential questions from friends and classmates about your extra help.

Who Is on Your Team and What Will They Do?

Take a look at the following sentences. They describe some thoughts or ideas that kids might have about the team of people helping them. Think about these statements and decide whether you think they are *true* or *false*.

1. I know who is on my team.   ◯ TRUE ◯ FALSE

If you answered true, write the names of your team members here:

_____

_____

2. I know why each person is on my team.   ◯ TRUE ◯ FALSE

3. I know what each person will be doing to help me.   ◯ TRUE ◯ FALSE

4. I know what my role is on the team and how I can help myself.   ◯ TRUE ◯ FALSE

If you answered false, write the names of team members who can help you figure this out:

_____

5. I think it is a good thing that I have people to support me.   ◯ TRUE ◯ FALSE

If you answered false, who can you talk to about this?

_____

6. I think that I will get more homework
   because I have more teachers.　　　○ TRUE　○ FALSE

   If you answered true, how can you find out if this is
   really true for you?

   _____

7. I understand how the team members
   will keep track of how I'm doing.　　○ TRUE　○ FALSE

   If you answered false, it's okay to ask the adults on your
   team about this. Who can you ask and what can you say?

   _____

   _____

8. I know what my strengths and
   challenges are.　　　　　　　　　○ TRUE　○ FALSE

   If you answered false, pick a member of your team you
   can ask for help figuring out what your strengths and
   challenges are. Who will you ask for this help?

   _____

9. I know how to share my strengths
   with my team and I know how to
   ask for help when needed.　　　　○ TRUE　○ FALSE

My Strengths and Challenges

Sometimes it's hard to remember all of our strengths when we are having difficulties. We also sometimes forget that we need any help at all when things are going well. Fill out the two boxes below to help you remember your abilities and your challenges. Knowing what your challenges are is important because it helps you know what support you need. And focusing on your strengths can remind you that you are unique, have many abilities, and can build on these qualities.

STRENGTHS	CHALLENGES

CHAPTER 5

Succeeding with Your Plan

Since you now have a plan for getting help, everything should be great in school. Right? Well . . . maybe. But maybe not—at least, not yet. You might feel really relieved that you are getting the right kind of help for you. But just like teachers and other adults needed time to figure out how to help you, it sometimes takes a plan a while to work. Your plan may change a few times as your team learns what is best for you.

It may also take you a while to get used to your plan. And it can take some time for people around you to adjust, too. In this chapter, you'll learn more about how to handle many of your plan's details, challenges, and changes.

Before reading the rest of this chapter, go to pages 95–97 and answer the questions there about your plan.

Getting Used to Your New Schedule

You may have an IEP (Individualized Education Program) or a 504 plan. Maybe you have another type of plan. Whatever your plan looks like, it won't be exactly the same as another kid who gets special help. Your plan is right for **YOU.**

This plan may have changed your schedule a little. For example, you may still be in your regular classroom most of the time but leave once a day for the resource room. Or maybe your schedule is more like Gabby's or Hiromi's.

Gabby is 10 years old. She leaves the main classroom to get occupational therapy twice a week and speech therapy once a week.

Hiromi is 9 years old. He started going to the resource room every day. He spends 40 minutes there getting help with his reading and writing. He told his friend, "I meet with my special ed teacher and three other kids in my grade. I feel more relaxed there than I do in my big class. The work I do at the resource room is just right for me. It's not too hard, and not too easy. My only problem is that sometimes I miss stuff going on in my class."

If you leave your classroom to go to a resource room, speech therapy, occupational therapy, physical therapy, counseling, or other help, does your new schedule work for you? Your classroom teacher and your special education teachers will probably talk about the best time for you to leave the classroom. Even so, sometimes schedules need to be changed.

If your schedule works for you, that's wonderful. You may find that it's a relief to leave the larger classroom sometimes to get help designed specifically for you. But if you are missing a subject that is hard to make up or an activity you love, speak up. Your team won't know that you are uncomfortable unless you share your thoughts and feelings. That's why it's important for you to talk to an adult about any scheduling concerns that you have. It's helpful if you remember to speak up in a respectful and clear way. If you do this, you are being a **self-advocate**. That means you are trying to help yourself by calmly and clearly sharing your ideas and concerns with others. You can be proud of yourself for doing this. You are being part of the team by letting adults know how the new plan is working for you and how it might need to be changed.

If you do speak up, you may learn that your schedule can easily be changed to work better for you. Or, you may learn that the teachers can't find another time that works better. If this happens, it's okay to feel disappointed or even a little annoyed. But it's also important to then move forward and make the best of the situation. **What can you say to yourself to help you do this?**

Here are comments other kids have said to themselves as they try to accept a schedule that isn't perfect for them:

- "I like the group I'm in, even though I don't like the timing of my pull-out class."

- "I know they are trying to help me reach my goals, so I'll deal with it."

- "It won't last forever. They said they'll switch my time if something changes in their schedules."

- "My classroom teacher is great about helping me catch up on anything I miss. So it's really not that big of a deal after all."

Changes in Work and Tests

Have you noticed your work is a bit different since you started getting extra help? Many students in special education have work and tests modified to help them reach their goals. The changes you experience may be big or small. How do you feel about them? Here's how Kerin responded to her changes at first.

Kerin is 10 years old. One day she came home from school and told her mom, "I'm so mad. The teachers must think I can't do anything. I hate school." After she calmed down, Kerin explained, "My teachers give me math sheets with only 10 problems. Other kids get 20. My tests are shorter, too. Even my homework is different. What's wrong with me? Why did they do this to me?"

Later, Kerin learned that her different work didn't mean that there was anything wrong with her. And it didn't mean her teachers thought she wasn't smart. Kerin had something called a **learning disability,** or **LD.** Sometimes this name confuses or worries kids. Having a learning disability does *not* mean that you can't learn. It means that you learn differently from other kids. In fact, a better name is **learning difference.** There are many kinds of learning differences.

Kerin learned that:

• She has fewer math problems on each page because it is easier for her to focus on a problem and not get overwhelmed if problems are separated and in larger print.

• She has fewer total math problems so she can concentrate on certain skills. Rather than doing lots of problems, she focuses her time and learning on ones that teach her these specific skills.

• Her spelling words for homework are different from her classmates because her testing showed that she has difficulty putting letters and sounds together to read and spell words. So her spelling words target certain spelling rules that will help her learn to spell and read many more words.

- Her tests aren't that different. But she takes her tests in the resource room and she is given extra time. That way she can focus better and not feel rushed.

Kerin felt a lot better after she learned the reasons for these changes. If you aren't sure why you are getting different work or tests, ask. If you just assume the changes are because you can't learn, you may end up feeling frustrated and upset. So **ask questions** if you feel confused or unhappy about your changes. For example, you could ask your team exactly how your different work can help you reach your goals. Or you could ask why the changes to your tests are better for you.

Common Misunderstandings

When you start school each year, you probably have certain ideas about what your day and your work will be like. When you started your new plan, you probably also had certain ideas about how your day and work would change. It's natural to try to predict what will happen. But sometimes our predictions can lead us to expect situations that don't really happen. Here are two common misunderstandings many kids have about their new plans.

"I thought school would be easier now." Bobby is 11 years old. He started going to the resource room a few months ago. He also started seeing a speech therapist. Bobby thought school would be easy for him once he got this help. He was upset and disappointed when he still had trouble with some of his work. He told his father, "Why is this still so hard? Plus, I think I'm doing even more work than I did before. I still get work from my regular teacher. And now I get *extra* work from my resource room teacher. That's not fair."

Bobby's questions are common. He met with his resource room teacher and his parents to talk about his confusion. His teacher understood Bobby's frustration. She explained, "It's true that you are doing challenging work. If it were easy, that would mean you were working on things you *already* do well. We don't want to waste your time with tasks that won't help you learn better. Instead, we are giving you work that will help you reach your goals. This work focuses on building the specific skills that you are struggling with."

The teacher also told Bobby that he was improving. She said, "It sounds like you have noticed that your work still seems hard. But what you might not have noticed is that you are doing a better job with it than you did a few months ago. You're doing it more quickly, too. How do you feel about that?"

Bobby admitted that he was learning a lot. He said, "The special work still scares me a little. But it used to be super hard for me." After the meeting, Bobby understood more about his plan. And he felt better about continuing to work on his skills.

Like Bobby, you have probably learned that you are getting work that is right for you. That might mean that your special education teacher spends a lot of time helping you focus on areas that are hard for you. This may not always be fun. But it *will* make it easier for you to reach your goals. Your special education teacher is there to support you and guide you if you feel confused or stressed.

"I'll never catch up with the work my friends are doing."
Sometimes kids worry that if some of their work is different, they may miss out on things that they really need to learn in their grade. Kids' parents might be concerned about this, too.

If you have this worry, remember that **there is no one right way to learn lessons or information.** If you work hard, focus on your plan and goals, and study the material, then you should be moving in the right direction. Plus, your teachers will help you learn the information you need. They don't want you to fall behind either. But if you do feel that you aren't learning certain important lessons, speak up. You will read about the importance of speaking up a lot in this book. That's because keeping thoughts and feelings a secret means that you are keeping other people from understanding you. Tell other people what you are worried about. See if you and your team can brainstorm ways to make sure you get the work that you need in order to move forward.

Telling Others About Your Plan

Kids are often curious about any changes their friends or classmates make. It's natural for kids to want to know where a friend goes when he leaves the classroom. Are they being nosy? You may think they are . . . and they might be, sometimes. But mostly, they probably just want to know if they are missing out on something fun. Or they may just miss having you in class!

Have you spent time thinking about what you want to say if someone asks you questions about where you are going and why? Here are some quick tips and ideas:

- If you seem okay with talking about your special help, others probably won't think it's a big deal.

- Answer the questions honestly, but don't worry about explaining everything about your IEP. If someone asks where you are going, you can say "occupational therapy" if that's where you are headed. If they ask why, you can just say "to work on my handwriting," or some other reply based on what you do there.

- Remember that **it's important to get the right help for you and your learning style.** Knowing that you are making good decisions for your future can help you be positive when others ask questions.

- Act casual when you leave your classroom. That way, others won't think you are embarrassed or that you dread going to your special help.

- If you aren't sure how to handle a specific question or situation, you can ask an adult you trust for suggestions or advice. Teachers have probably talked with lots of children who have received help. They may be able to give you advice that has worked for other students.

Sometimes kids may tease people who act, look, think, feel, or do things differently from them. Have you ever been teased? Or have you ever teased others? A lot of times, teasing is not the same as bullying. Sometimes teasing is really another word for joking (that accidentally upsets another person). Teasing can really hurt. If a friend you trust teases you, you may just laugh or calmly say, "Hey, that's not funny." You know the friend isn't trying to be mean. But if another kid says the same thing, you may feel hurt or embarrassed.

If someone does start saying hurtful things about your special work, what can you do and say? Here are three important guidelines:

- **Act confident, casual, and cool.** Kids tend to tease more if they get a big reaction from you. (If you need help doing this, take a look at Positive Attitude Tool #2: Find Ways to Feel Calm on page 31.)

- **Do what you need to do.** It's okay to leave at your scheduled time, even if others notice. You are making a smart decision to get the help you need.

- **Say something that is quick, informative, and comfortable for you** if anyone asks you questions or teases you.

If you need help remembering these guidelines, remind yourself of the word **ADS**. Each letter in this word can remind you of one key point: **A** for "Act confident," **D** for "Do what you need to do," and **S** for "Say what you feel is a comfortable explanation if anyone asks where you are going."

Many students who get special education don't deal with teasing, but they might still worry about it happening. For example, **Fatima** is 13 years old. She hasn't been teased. But she often worries about what her friends think. When she learned she needed to get occupational therapy and speech and language therapy, and also go to the resource room, she was upset. She thought her social life was over.

Then Fatima spoke with her neighbor, Maria. Maria is two years older than Fatima. She has a lot of friends. And she also gets extra help.

After talking with Maria, Fatima found out that she could just simply and clearly explain what was going on to her friends. If she did this in a matter-of-fact way, like it's no big deal, her friends would probably be okay with it. That's exactly what happened. First she told her best friend, Grace. Grace just nodded and said, "Cool." Grace didn't really ask many questions after that. She knows that Fatima is nice, funny, and smart. Plus, she and Fatima share a lot of the same interests. These are the things Grace feels are important.

Some kids do deal with teasing sometimes. **Sean** is 11 years old. He likes to joke around and he has lots of friends. Sean started going to the resource room each day. Two kids began teasing him about leaving the classroom. Sean was scared that the whole class would start making fun of him. He thought about just staying in class and never going to the resource room again. But he wanted the extra help. He knew it was useful. So he tried to come up with another solution.

Remember the ADS guidelines? Sean used them to deal with the situation he was facing.

A: Act confident, casual, and cool.

When Sean's classmates teased him about having to get extra help, Sean wanted to show that he was confident. He shrugged his shoulders, stayed calm, and said, "I learn best when I work with Mrs. Johnson. Cool, huh?"

D: Do what you need to do.

Sean decided that he would just get up and leave class as casually as he could when it was time for his resource room help. He didn't make a big deal about leaving. He also talked to his resource room teacher about the teasing. She gave him some more do's and don'ts. She said:

- **Do** ignore the teasing if you can.

- **Do** smile if you think the teasing is just a joke.

- **Do** talk to an adult later if the teasing doesn't stop or is really bothering you.

- **Don't** tease back, even if you feel upset, hurt, or angry.

- **Don't** believe the teasing words just because the kid is popular or because you usually look up to him or her.

- **Don't** decide to stop getting help because another kid is saying unkind things to you.

S: Say something that is quick, informative, and comfortable for you.

Sean likes to tell jokes and make people laugh. So he decided to try responding with a quick joke. When one kid kept teasing him about leaving class, Sean smiled. Then he said, "Wow, I feel like a superstar, the way you notice everything I do!" The comment worked to stop this kid from teasing him. Another time, a different kid accused him of going to a teacher who gave him answers to work and tests. That time, Sean smiled and said, "I wish." He calmly explained that he didn't get work or test answers at his other class. But he said that he liked the class because it helped him understand math. Sean also knew that another option was to say nothing. He could have just ignored the comment.

If you want a reminder of the ADS guidelines, turn to page 98. You can photocopy this form, or print a copy from freespirit.com/special-ed. Then you can keep this reminder with you and look at it whenever you want to.

Responding to Teasing

In this section, you will learn more about how to handle teasing. Many students are *not* teased because of their extra help. Even if you are not teased about school, keep reading this section anyway. These ideas can help you respond to teasing about anything. But we will talk specifically about teasing related to your special education help.

If you are teased, it can feel really bad. Remind yourself that **you have nothing to be embarrassed about** just because you need some extra help. After all, don't all people need help at some time? Think about it. Kids who are too young to drive need help getting places that are too far to travel to by foot or on bicycle, for example. And adults ask for help from specialists like doctors, plumbers, electricians, and lawyers when they need help with things they are not experts in. So there's no reason you should feel bad about accepting help from a special teacher.

If friends ever tease you or make jokes that bother you, one response is to find a quiet time to talk. Be honest. Say that you are uncomfortable with what your friends have been saying. Tell them that you want them to stop. If they are truly your friends, they will likely respect your request. Be sure that you don't tease your friends back, though. That will not solve the situation. And it may even lead to your friends teasing you again.

If other kids say things that bother you, the chart on the next page shows examples of some responses you might be able to use. Some students have found that answers like these worked for them when they were being teased. You can change these responses to work for you. Not every response will be right for every situation. You may also want to talk with your parents or teachers about ideas for how you can handle teasing. If someone keeps teasing, or if someone bullies you, get help from a grownup you trust.

Remember, if you respond with confidence, you are less likely to be teased. If you feel comfortable, you can also joke around (without teasing back). Or you can explain your situation to kids who might be teasing because they are confused about special education. But if you *are* teased (even after trying to ignore it), speak up. If you aren't sure how to deal with the situation, **ask a trusted adult for help.** You don't need to accept being teased.

I learn best in my other classroom.

Teasing or Other Comments That Might Bother You	Possible Responses
"How come you keep going to that other room?"	"It's easier for me to learn there." "I like it because it's not so noisy."
"What do you do in the other room?"	"I work!" "We go over a lot of math. I learn new ways to do it. It's fun!"
"How come you have four teachers?"	"They are experts in four different areas. No big deal." "I'm just lucky, I guess!"
"You only do well because you get a different test."	"It looks different, but it covers the same information." "I do well because I work really hard."
"How come you're reading baby books?"	"I like reading shorter books." "I learn them to read to my little cousin." "I'm awesome at the trumpet, but I read slowly. These books help me learn to read faster."
"We don't want you in our group. You take too long to write."	"Okay. But you'll miss out on a lot. I may write kind of slowly, but I think fast. And I have great ideas."

Quick and Helpful Hints

In this chapter, you read a lot about how to make your plan work for you. You found out how to understand changes to your schedule, work, and tests. This chapter also focused on how you can deal with questions or teasing from other kids.

Here are some of this chapter's important ideas:

- Starting your new school plan can be a great step. But it may take some time to get used to it.

- Getting the right help doesn't mean getting easy work. It means getting work that will help you reach your goals.

- If you discover that you are missing something important while you're in extra help, let the teachers know. They may be able to find a solution. But your teachers can't help if they don't know that there is a problem.

- Remember the **ADS** guidelines. How you Act, what you Do, and what you Say can show others that you are comfortable and confident with your new plan and with yourself.

In the next chapter, you will learn how to focus on your abilities, not just on your challenges. You will get the chance to explore how to be kind to yourself and not demand perfection. In addition, you will read about ways that working hard to achieve realistic goals can lead to pride and confidence.

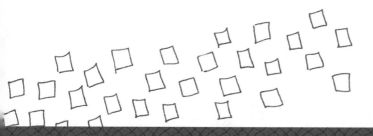

How Are You Adjusting to Your Plan?

Answer the following questions about you, your schoolwork, and your friendships.

1. Has your school schedule changed
   because of your plan? ○ YES ○ NO

   If you answered yes, does the new
   schedule work for you? ○ YES ○ NO

   If the schedule isn't working well, why not? Who can you
   talk with about adjusting it so it works better?

   _____

   _____

2. Has your team made changes to some
   of your work, homework, and tests? ○ YES ○ NO

   If you answered yes, are the
   changes helpful? ○ YES ○ NO

   If you answered no, who can you talk to about this?

   _____

3. Do you understand why you are
   getting the help you are? ○ YES ○ NO

4. Do you know what your goals are during
   your time with your extra help teacher? ○ YES ○ NO

   If you answered no, who can you talk to about this?

   _____

If you answered yes, write down some goals you are working to reach.

_____

_____

5. Do you understand how the help you are receiving can help you reach your goals? ◯ YES ◯ NO

   If you answered no, ask! It's important to know how your extra help is supposed to support you.

6. Do you ever feel like you're still struggling even though you're getting help? ◯ YES ◯ NO

   If you answered yes, share your concerns with an adult. Who can you talk to about this?

   _____

7. Do you know how you can quickly explain your extra help to your friends and other people? ◯ YES ◯ NO

   If you answered yes, write down your explanation here:

   _____

   _____

   If you answered no, who could you talk with about ideas for how to explain?

   _____

8. Do you know what to say if friends or
   other kids ask why some of your work
   is different from what they do?   ○ YES   ○ NO

   If you answered yes, write one thing you can say:

   _____

   _____

   If you answered no, who could you talk to about
   what to say?

   _____

9. If you are comfortable getting extra help,
   it will probably be easier for your friends
   to be okay with it, too. Do you mostly
   feel good about getting extra help?   ○ YES   ○ NO

   If you answered no, who can you talk to about this?

   _____

10. Has anyone ever teased you about
    getting extra help or special education? ○ YES   ○ NO

    If you answered yes, do you know good
    ways to respond to the teasing to make
    it stop?   ○ YES   ○ NO

    If you answered no, it's time to speak to an adult. You
    shouldn't be teased because you are getting the right
    help for you. Which adult could you speak with?

    _____

Using ADS

Remember, if you face questions or teasing about getting special education—or about anything else—you can use the ADS guidelines to handle these situations.

A: Act casual, cool, and confident.

Kids tend to tease more if they get a big reaction from you. So do your best to stand tall and stay calm.

D: Do what you need to do.

Remember that you are making a smart decision to get the help you need, and don't let teasing stop you from getting the help you need. If teasing doesn't stop or is really bothering you, talk to an adult.

S: Say something that is quick, informative, and comfortable for you if anyone asks you questions or teases you.

You might respond with a quick joke or a simple explanation. Or you can say nothing and ignore the comment if that's most comfortable for you.

CHAPTER 6

Focusing on Your Abilities

Wherever you are in the process of getting special education, you have probably been working hard at things that are challenging for you. But it's important to remember that your challenges are not what make you special. They are not what make you **YOU.** There is a lot more to you than your difficulties. And it is important not to forget about all your strengths, talents, and skills. This chapter is about how you can stay positive and focus on these areas. Before reading the rest of the chapter, go to page 114 and think about the sentences there.

Six Steps for Being a Positive, Confident You

Life can be pretty stressful when you worry a lot about why you have challenges and what you can do about them. It is important to focus on improving areas that are hard for you. But it is just as important to focus on your abilities.

To help you do this, this chapter will talk about six big steps. These steps can help you learn ways to feel positive about yourself and your skills. You can use these steps even while you're working to improve in your areas of difficulty.

As you read about these six steps, you may be tempted to skip over some of them. But try to go step-by-step without missing any. Each step is important.

Before you start, it might be helpful to read about how another student felt after he used the steps. Here's what William had to say.

William is 8 years old. He told his brother, "At first, I thought the six steps were a stupid idea. I didn't want to do any of them. But my therapist made me think about this stuff. I'm glad he did. I didn't expect any of these ideas to work, but they really do. I feel a lot better about myself and about getting my special help now."

Step #1: Focus on the Positive

Have you ever cheered up a friend who was feeling sad? Maybe you did this by reminding that friend how great he or she is. Good friends do this for each other. Confident people also do this for themselves—and you can, too.

First, take a few minutes to **think of at least three positive qualities about yourself.** These qualities shouldn't be about what you can do well. You'll think about that next. Right now, think about your personality. Can you think of three great things about your personality? You can write them on notebook paper. Or you can type them on a computer and print out your list. You can also have an adult help you type or write the list. Then keep this list in a place where you can look at it often.

If you have trouble coming up with three special qualities, look over the following list. Which words describe you? Feel free to use different words if you have qualities that aren't on this list.

athletic   patient   trustworthy   cooperative

creative   honest   considerate   insightful

happy   responsible   funny   sensitive

positive   generous   respectful   outgoing

brave   gentle   awesome   sweet

thoughtful

confident   energetic   courageous

caring   helpful   unique   smart

studious   fair-minded   kind   loving

Now, add some areas of talent or ability to your list. Maybe you really enjoy one of these activities or are really talented in one of these areas:

This list does not cover every talent that people could have. Write (or type) what your talents are, even if they are not on this list. Then, keep paying attention to things you're good at. Whenever you notice one of your talents, skills, or special qualities, add it to your growing list. It can also be helpful (or just fun) to ask family, friends, teachers, or other people you trust what positive words they would use to describe you. Add those words to your list. Look at your list whenever you need reminders of all the great and special qualities that make up *you*. That's what Brooke did.

Brooke is 9 years old. She is the youngest kid in her family. She complained to her dad that her brothers and sisters were smarter and more talented than she was. They also seemed to have more freedom to do what they wanted. She added, "The other kids in my class are smarter and more popular than me, too. And they get better grades."

Brooke's dad reminded her that her teacher had suggested that she make a list of her special qualities. Brooke sometimes focused on others and their abilities rather than focusing on what made her special. Brooke sat down in her room and came up with her list. She later said that it was helpful to focus on positive words that describe her. She also asked friends and family to share what they liked about her. Brooke told her dad, "It was fun when everyone said such great things about me!" After Brooke finished writing her list, she took the information and wrote a few sentences about herself. She wrote:

"My name is Brooke. Here's what's great about me: I'm funny, loving, smart in math, kind, a good friend, and outgoing. I love swimming. And I'm pretty good at making things out of clay!"

Brooke took what she wrote and taped it to her desk at home. She looked at it whenever she felt sad or discouraged. She discovered that it helped her focus on the positive. One of her friends saw it in her room and said, "That's pretty cool! I'm going to try it, too."

Step #2: Be Kind to Yourself

In Step 1, you came up with a list of great things about yourself. How do you feel when you read the list? In other words, do you appreciate your special qualities and skills? Do you smile when you think about what makes you a unique person?

You can **be kind to yourself by remembering your abilities and talents.** Be sure to do this even when things are tough. In fact, it is *especially* important to be kind to yourself at those times.

Of course, everyone has bad days when it is hard to focus on the positive qualities. Maybe you are struggling with a homework assignment that seems easy for your friend. Or you might have baked a cake that came out lopsided. On days like this, can you still feel good about your abilities? If you struggle to stay positive during difficult times, try some of these ideas for being kind to yourself.

- Admit that you wished for a different outcome. It's okay to feel disappointed when things don't go as you had hoped. But it's important to remind yourself that you are still a great person.

- Remember that one disappointment does not represent who you are. One difficulty does not define you or explain who you are as a person. You will have disappointments and challenges. Everyone has them. But these difficulties don't take away from all your abilities. Remember that your abilities are part of you no matter what challenges you currently have to deal with.

- Learn from the experience. Use it to set new goals for the future. At the same time, try to feel proud of what you tried and what you did.

- Laugh *with* yourself. We all mess up sometimes. But try not to laugh *at* yourself. That can hurt. Laughing

with yourself is like saying, "Oops! Oh well. I may have made a silly mistake, but who cares? It really was a little funny." Laughing *at* yourself is like someone teasing or bullying you.

• Ask friends, family members, or teachers for tips on how they stay positive when they face challenges.

Step #3: Believe That Hard Work Pays Off . . . *Really*

Lots of kids roll their eyes when adults say, "Hard work pays off." So, before you roll *your* eyes and skip this section, hang on!

Putting in a lot of effort definitely *can* pay off. But maybe it hasn't always worked that way for you in the past. If you try a plan over and over again and it doesn't lead to success, you are still working hard. But it's only leading to frustration. You probably need a new plan—one that gets you closer to reaching your goals.

You also don't need to focus only on tasks that are difficult for you. You may find it pays off to work hard in areas that you are already talented in. Think about Jeremy's story.

Jeremy is 11 years old. He loves base-ball. But when he was getting ready to try out for his school's team, he didn't practice batting much. He figured he was already good enough at hitting. Instead, he spent time practicing his pitching. When he tried out for the baseball team, he was surprised to learn that he didn't make it. The coach told him, "I need well-rounded players. They have to put in the time to build up *all* their abilities. You're a great pitcher. But I need you to be able to hit for the team, too."

Jeremy was disappointed. But he didn't give up. He decided to focus on the positive. And he came up with a new plan. Jeremy told himself, "I'm already a good pitcher. Actually, the coach used the word *great*! I know that I can improve my hitting if I work hard." After working on his pitching, he had gotten a lot better. His math skills had also improved because of the work he did with his resource room teacher. So Jeremy decided to keep practicing his pitching. But now he also spent time going to the batting cage. His skills started to improve. He felt proud. And he was happy to see the results of his efforts.

Guess what happened the next season at baseball try-outs? Jeremy made the team! His coach said, "You have great pitching skills. We still need to work on your batting some more. But I can see that you really tried hard. Your batting is better than it was last year. Congratulations!"

Working hard doesn't mean you will have instant success. And it doesn't mean you'll be able to figure out how to do everything by yourself. Working hard *does* mean that you are willing to put in time to improve and that you are willing to try different ways to improve. It means asking for help when you need it. And it means feeling proud that you have the courage to keep trying. (This idea is also called **perseverance.** You will learn more about it in Chapter 7.)

Step #4: Remember That No One Is Perfect

Have you ever looked around your class and thought, "That kid has it all together. He's perfect!"? Or maybe you've looked at a friend and thought, "She just does everything right." You might be surprised to learn that many kids have these thoughts about others. Even some adults feel like a coworker "knows everything" or a friend "never struggles with anything."

Here's the truth: **No one is perfect.** And remembering this will help you accept yourself when you make a mistake or don't do something perfectly. Instead of thinking that there is something wrong with you, you can remind yourself that you are human. That means that you *and* everyone you know will make mistakes and not be perfect at everything or on every day. So, why put pressure on *yourself* to be perfect? Here's what Aviva experienced.

Aviva is 12 years old. Her friends often tell her she's "perfect." Aviva just laughs, because she knows this isn't true. One day her best friend, Shoshanna, told Aviva, "I wish I could be perfect like you." That's when Aviva decided to tell her friend a secret. She said, "I don't think I'm smarter than anybody else. But I *do* know how to ask for help when I need it. I'm not afraid to get extra help for math—I go see Mr. Greenberg every day for help. And you know what? I still can't quite figure out how to ride a bike. But I feel really good about being me. I'm okay with what I can do, and what I still struggle to learn. So that's my big secret—confidence!"

Shoshanna thought her friend was perfect. But really, Aviva was showing confidence. She accepted herself—with all of her abilities *and* her difficulties. Because Aviva didn't seem bothered about getting math help in the resource room, Shoshanna didn't see it as a negative, either. She saw it as a sign of Aviva being serious about learning.

Confidence plays a big part in how other people see you. And it's easier to be confident when you remember that no one is perfect. This can help you laugh at your mistakes rather than feeling disappointed or embarrassed. And it can help you feel better about getting extra help.

If you feel like you have to be perfect all the time, think about this: Even Olympic athletes, who are some of the best in the world at their sports, aren't perfect. In the Olympics, ice skaters sometimes fall and runners sometimes trip. If you worry a lot about being perfect, talk about this with someone you trust.

Step #5: Keep Trying When Things Are Hard

We all run into obstacles and difficulties. We all fail or make mistakes sometimes. These mistakes don't mean that we can't eventually succeed at a task. They simply mean that we need to keep trying. **What's most important is how we handle the difficulty.**

It can be tempting to give up when we feel discouraged. And it's true that some goals are impossible. When you were younger, did you ever try to fly by flapping your arms? No matter how hard you worked at that goal, it would never happen. Try to set goals that are possible and realistic. And as you work toward your goals, take pride in improvements you make along the way.

As you work on not giving up, it can help to think about how you usually handle challenging events. Do you feel easily defeated? Or do you remember that you have lots of positive qualities, even when you're struggling with something? Think about the following situations and pick the choice that is closest to how you would probably respond.

1. You and a friend both play a video game for the first time. You lose in Level 1. Your friend easily makes it to Level 4. You:

   (a) Think, "I'm terrible at this. I'll never get better at this game no matter how hard I try. I'm never playing this game again."

   (b) Want to buy the game to get better at it. Even so, you doubt that you'll ever get past Level 1.

   (c) Plan to ask your friend for tips on how to improve. Then you'll play the game again to see if you can come up with even more ideas.

2. Your teacher gives your class a week to complete a homework assignment. You have to write about your hero and then read your essay in class on the due date. When it is time to share, all the kids at your table have three or four paragraphs written about their heroes. You only wrote three sentences. You:

   (a) Think, "I know I stink at writing, and this proves it! I'll have to find a way to leave the classroom before it's time for everyone to read their essays."

   (b) Tell the other kids, and your teacher, that you had a lot of things to do after school this week. You say that's why you didn't have time to write more. Then you read your three sentences aloud.

   (c) Tell kids, and your teacher, that you think of great ideas but have a hard time writing essays. You also ask for tips on how others write, so that you might be able to write more easily next time.

3. You like to run, and have always thought you were fast. Your older brother is on the track team. He says you should think about trying out. So you decide to go to

a practice and see what it's like. At practice, the coach times everyone running 500 meters and then a mile. You come in 6th place out of 13 in the 500 meter, and last place in the mile. You:

(a) Think, "I obviously can't run fast when it really counts. My brother's idea was stupid. I'm never going back there again."

(b) Feel embarrassed. You wonder whether you could ever be fast enough to make the team. But you decide you'll go back to the track to try to beat your times.

(c) Remind yourself that you are a hard worker. And now you feel really motivated to improve your times. You decide you'll still try out for the team. If you make it, you'll learn from your teammates and coach. You feel confident that you could be faster by the end of the season.

How did you answer these questions? If you gave some "a" answers, you may sometimes give up when you run into challenges. If that's true, it's important to find ways to build your confidence and stay motivated. If you responded with some "b" answers, you learn from your experiences. You probably feel okay about yourself, even when you face obstacles. If you gave some "c" answers, then you know it's okay to admit that you are not perfect. You probably also know how to set goals and work toward them.

When you feel good about yourself, you're able to handle challenges more easily. You are more likely to find the strength to keep trying and not give up. And you feel proud of your efforts. Here are a few tips on how to keep trying and not give up:

• Check on whether your goal is possible. You might want to talk this through with an adult. If your goal is reachable, remind yourself of that. If it isn't, work on setting a new goal.

- Remind yourself of your abilities so you don't get too discouraged or upset with yourself when you can't succeed immediately.

- Most people have to work to get better at things. Remind yourself that you may feel frustrated but that is not always a reason to stop trying or to get mad at yourself.

- Remember that it's okay to ask for help. If you are getting really frustrated, then it's time to calmly ask for the specific support that would help you.

- Rather than trying to reach a huge goal right away, try reaching a smaller goal that can eventually lead to the bigger one. For example, you could work on playing a scale on the piano before playing a difficult song.

You might discover that you feel excited about taking on the challenge of learning something new or reaching a goal. It can also be fun to pay attention to your improvements along the way. These can help you stay motivated and positive as you work through obstacles.

Step #6: Show Your Confidence

It's great to feel confident. It can mean that you aren't too nervous to take on new experiences, because you believe you can handle them or you can comfortably ask for help. And **showing your confidence can let others know that you value yourself and like being you.** But many kids are not sure how to share their talents with others without sounding like they are bragging. (Some adults have trouble with this, too.) Here are some great ways to let your friends, teachers, and other people know that you are happy being you:

- Smile!
- Stand or sit up straight and tall.
- Make eye contact with other people. (But remember not to stare.)

- Expect that most people will like you.

- Honestly compliment others on *their* abilities.

- Accept compliments from others. You deserve credit for your strengths.

- Share your interests and talents with others so they know about what you like and what you do well. But try not to brag. For example, instead of saying, "I'm great at archery!" you could say, "One of my hobbies is archery. What do you like to do?"

- Show that you are comfortable asking for help.

- Show that you can bounce back from mistakes or tough times. Sometimes it's hard to do this after something difficult happens in your life. But you can take steps to help yourself. For example, asking others for support is a sign of strength and courage. So is spending time focusing on what is relaxing or fun for you. Even if you can't do this right away because you feel stressed or upset, it's a goal to strive for when you are ready.

- Try not to put yourself down, either out loud or in your mind. If you do, it's okay to tell yourself, "Putting myself down doesn't help. I need to be my own best friend and be kind to myself instead."

Think about people you know who seem confident. Pay attention to how they act and talk. You will probably notice that they do many of the things you just read about. You may spot other confident things they do, too. Next, give it a try yourself—*act* confident. It can help you eventually *feel* confident.

Quick and Helpful Hints

In this chapter, you learned six steps to becoming a more positive, confident you. Using these skills and ideas can help you feel better about your abilities and about yourself. These steps can also help you find learning less stressful because you know that you don't have to be perfect, and you know that you are an important person even if you struggle in some areas.

Here are some important ideas to remember after reading this chapter:

- Life is less stressful when you can feel confident and positive, even when you face challenges.

- Some of the ways that you can stay positive include being kind to yourself, remembering that no one is perfect, and being willing to work hard and keep trying when things are difficult.

- If you act more confident, you may start to feel more confident.

In the next chapter you will learn even more tools for becoming a confident, successful you. The tips you will read about can help you in school and even later in life when you are an adult.

Do You Celebrate Your Strengths?

Think about the following sentences. Put a check mark next to the ones that already describe you.

○ Most of the time, I feel good about myself and my abilities.

○ I know my areas of talent.

○ I have shared my strengths with adults.

○ I know how to share my talents with other kids without bragging.

○ I work on getting even better at things I'm good at already.

○ I believe that my friends, family, and teachers know about my strengths.

○ I know that some of my strengths have to do with my personality, not just with things I can do.

○ If I'm feeling down about myself, I can think about my abilities and feel a little better.

○ I don't judge my friends negatively just because they don't have the same talents I do.

○ I am willing to help my friends in areas I know a lot about. I know that everyone needs help sometimes.

How many of the sentences did you check? It's okay if you are just beginning to think about some of these ideas. Maybe you have been working to understand your challenges. Maybe you have been focusing on your new plan and your goals. That is hard work. You might feel like you have not had much time to focus on the special qualities you are proud of, and the things you enjoy. Now is the time!

CHAPTER 7

Eight Important Ingredients for Success

Throughout this book, you've learned a lot about yourself, your special education help, your plan, and more. In this chapter, you'll learn eight great ingredients for success. These tips and tools have helped lots of kids, teens, and adults do their best and reach their goals. These tips won't make a learning difficulty go away. And they won't magically solve every challenge you may face. But if you learn to use these skills, you may find that you are happier, less stressed, and more successful in school and beyond. Before reading the rest of this chapter, go to page 138 to think more about this.

Ingredient #1: Perseverance

Perseverance is a big word. But its meaning is pretty simple. If you show perseverance, it means you don't give up. You keep trying to succeed. You *persevere*. Have you ever heard this phrase?

If at first you don't succeed, try, try again.

This saying is about perseverance.

Alex, age 10, knew that one of his strengths was that he persevered. He told his parents, "When I first tried to learn long division, I wanted to give up. But I didn't. I told myself that I might get it if I just kept trying. I asked the teacher for help. I asked both of you for help. I even asked my friends for help. Then I kept practicing what everyone taught me. I'm so glad I kept working. Check out my test grade!" Alex smiled and handed his parents his test paper from his long division test in class. His parents were happy that Alex's test grade reflected his understanding of the work. They were even happier about his ability to persevere even when he was frustrated. Alex was courageous to persevere and keep trying.

Sticking with a challenge is an important quality that successful people have. But sometimes, refusing to give up can make things harder. It's important to figure out when you should keep trying your strategy for succeeding at a task and when to switch to another plan. Consider Jamie's story.

Jamie is 11 years old. She wanted to make a robot from a kit her parents bought for her. Jamie looked at the pictures in the directions. She tried to follow them. But she struggled to put two of the pieces together.

She tried over and over. Jamie spent hours trying to force the pieces to go together. Jamie was upset. She didn't understand why she hadn't succeeded. She told her mom, "I kept trying and didn't give up. So why couldn't I figure it out? I think they must have put the wrong pieces in the box. I'm so upset!"

Jamie *did* persevere. She kept working on her strategy for building the robot. But in this case, working hard only led to frustration for Jamie. She didn't succeed. Why not?

Persevering does not only mean that you work hard and stick with a task. It also means that if you get stuck, you think about ways to get *un*stuck. Sometimes we just keep trying the same thing over and over even though it isn't working. That's what happened to Jamie. When Jamie's plan didn't work the first couple of times, she needed a *new* plan. Maybe the two pieces she thought should fit together really belonged in other places on the robot. Maybe she needed to take a closer look at the instructions. Or she could have decided to ask someone for help.

When *you* get stuck, try thinking of new ideas. Maybe you look over the instructions for your homework again. You might need to try a different way to solve a math problem or read a map from your social studies class. Maybe the task isn't a right match for your skills right now. At rare times, there *may* even be an error in the material you have. It's possible that the kit that Jamie used really was missing a piece.

Speak up and ask questions if you aren't sure how to complete a project or an assignment. Other people may be able to offer you ideas on how to keep working with a different approach.

> **Persevering at a strategy that doesn't work can be exhausting. To get unstuck, try a new strategy.**

Perseverance does *not* mean that you have to do everything on your own. You may decide to ask a parent or teacher for help. For example, here's what Hector did.

Hector is 13 years old. He takes his schoolwork very seriously. He also works hard at soccer. When he has a problem with a topic in class or with a play in soccer, he tries really hard to figure things out. If he still feels confused after trying something on his own, he knows that he can turn to his teacher or coach for guidance. Doing this helps him get the support he needs. That way, he can keep working hard to improve his skills.

At times, you might find it hard to persevere. If you feel bored, frustrated, tired, or anxious, you may want to give up. It might seem like it's just too hard to keep working. If you ever feel this way, try taking a break. Focus on the challenge again later in the day. Or you might even wait until another day when you are ready to persevere again.

Here are some tips on how to persevere:

- Compliment yourself for working hard, even when the task is difficult.

- If you get frustrated when you keep trying one plan, try to find a new plan to reach your goal.

- Remember that it's okay to ask for advice or help if you get stuck.

- If you feel like you can't keep working, take a break. Pick another time to focus on the task again.

Ingredient #2: Organization

Being organized is a very useful skill. It can help you figure out how to fit all of your activities and responsibilities into your schedule. It can also help you plan what you need to do now, and what can wait until later. That way you're less likely to end up overwhelmed and anxious when time is running out before a test or project.

Jayesh is 11 years old. He admits, "I used to just stuff all of my schoolwork into my backpack. It seemed like it saved me time. But one day at school, kids started complaining that my backpack smelled funny. I was really embarrassed. When I got home, I dumped everything out of my bag. That's how I found the reason for the smell. I'd left a banana in the bottom and it was rotting. I didn't even remember putting it in my backpack. From that day on, I decided to get organized."

Jayesh asked his mother to help him get organized. First, they put all of his papers into the right folders. Science papers went into the science folder, music sheets went into the music folder, and so on. Next, Jayesh wrote the subjects on the covers of his notebooks so he knew quickly if he had the right or wrong notebook for a class. Jayesh also knew that he was always rushing to leave at the end of the day. So he and his mom put one purple folder in his backpack. It was a place where he could temporarily put all loose papers. Then, at home, Jayesh would go through that folder and put the papers where they belonged.

At first, it took Jayesh a while to get used to this new system. But he grew to like it. In fact, later he started teaching his

younger brother how to get organized, too. Jayesh said, "It saves me time when I'm studying. I know where everything is and I'm more relaxed. I don't worry that I've lost things. It's so much better than before!"

Do you struggle with organization? Maybe you don't know how or where to start. It can seem complicated to keep track of all your homework, test dates, long-term projects, social plans, and family activities. Here are some tips for getting organized and staying that way:

- Use a homework notebook to write down homework assignments. This way you don't have to remember every detail. If you need to double-check something, it's easy to look at your notebook.

- At home, use a monthly calendar (sometimes called a month-at-a-glance calendar). Write all of your project due dates and test dates on the calendar. You might want to put project dates in one color and test dates in another.

- Work on identifying the parts of each of your projects, and the topics for each of your tests. List these items as separate due dates on your calendar. This way, on each date, you only do a small piece of the project or a single chunk of studying.

- Also include activities, such as your basketball games, on your calendar. This will help you remember them and remind you to set aside time to do more homework on other nights. Your calendar can be on paper or on a computer or tablet.

- Have a folder for each school subject (science, social studies, and so on). Put handouts, graded tests, homework assignments, and other

Being organized can save you time and energy.

subject-specific items in these folders. You can also have a folder for miscellaneous things like school newsletters, letters for your parents, and so on.

- Organize areas like your locker at school, your desk at home, and your schoolbag. This can help you save time looking for things.

- Remember, taking a little time to get organized now can save you a lot of stress later on.

These strategies have helped many other kids. They might work for you, too.

Sofia is 12 years old. She found out that she really liked breaking up assignments and doing only a little each night. She said, "It takes a few extra minutes when I first get the assignment, but I make sure I do only a little bit of the work at a time so I don't get too tired or bored. I did my essay on the Civil War this way. First, I used a graphic organizer to list the topics I wanted to write about. The next night, I wrote my opening paragraph. Then I still had five nights before the essay was due. I spent the next three nights writing two paragraphs each night on topics from my graphic organizer. The fourth night was when I wrote my last paragraph. The fifth night I edited the essay, and the next morning I handed it in. It wasn't too stressful when I organized my homework this way."

You may want to try a plan similar to the one Sofia used, or choose one of the tips listed earlier. If you want more ideas, ask your parents, teachers, siblings, or friends how they keep organized. Pick some ideas you think will work for you and give them a try. If they aren't right for you, try others.

Ingredient #3: Avoiding Procrastination

Has your parent ever told you to take out the garbage, do the dishes, or start your homework? Have you ever said, "I'll do it in a few minutes"? Two hours later, you may have forgotten about the garbage. Your parents might have needed to remind you several times to do the dishes. Or you might have put off your homework until it was late and you were too tired. This is called **procrastination.** When you procrastinate, you put off doing something until later. That might mean an hour later or a week later. Or you might *never* get around to doing it.

Of course, people *know* that putting off homework or chores won't make them disappear or finish themselves. So why do so many people procrastinate? There are two common reasons why kids procrastinate:

- They avoid the stress of doing the work right now.

- They feel that other activities are more important (or more fun).

Think about that first reason. Have you ever done this? Imagine that you put off studying for a math test. You feel nervous when you do the practice problems for the test. To avoid feeling that stress, you avoid studying. What do you think will happen on the day of the math test? You'll probably feel unprepared and nervous. And you might not be too proud of yourself for not studying.

Here's Michael's story of procrastination.

Michael is 11 years old. He had a month to work on his big social studies project. He was supposed to do research using several different sources. He also was supposed to create a digital presentation about the information that he gathered. Michael says, "The thought of doing the project stressed me out. And I always felt like I had too much else to do. So I kept putting it off. The night before the due date, I hadn't done anything. I panicked and started crying. I told my parents what was going on. At first they got mad. But then they tried to help me."

Michael's parents encouraged him to speak with his teacher as soon as he got to school the next morning. They suggested that he admit he had waited too long to begin the project, and then ask for an extension. Meanwhile, Michael's parents helped him calm down and he started researching some information about his topic. After an hour of work, Michael told his father, "This history is actually pretty interesting. I should have started doing it earlier."

What do you think happened for Michael? In the end, his teacher gave him a lower project grade because he did not hand it in on time. Michael felt embarrassed that his friends completed their work on time. However, he did eventually finish his project, and he felt proud that he had not given up. Michael was more motivated to get his work done on time in the future, because he didn't want to lose points just because he put off doing his work. He also never wanted to feel embarrassed again

> **Putting off some stress now can lead to more stress later.**

when his friends did the work and he didn't. Michael's teacher and parents also taught him helpful strategies to avoid procrastination on future projects.

The second common reason people procrastinate is because they have other things they need or want to focus on. Think about all the things you do. You might be involved in sports or other after-school activities. You probably hang out with friends and go to family get-togethers. You might have chores to do at home. You probably have nightly homework to do, plus hobbies you enjoy.

With all that going on, it can seem hard to squeeze in other responsibilities. You might have trouble finding the energy, focus, and time for big projects or studying for tests. And sometimes you may just want to play a game, read a book, go for a walk, or play with your cat instead of working. If this describes you, remember what you learned about Ingredient #2. **Organization is a very good way to help prevent procrastination.**

Sarah is 12 years old. She always felt that she was too busy to find time to do all of her homework. She was very popular, and she loved hanging out with her friends on social media, as well as going places with her friends and family. Sarah was also on two sports teams, took music lessons, and made sure to spend time doing chores and playing with her three dogs. She felt that she was a good friend and a responsible person. She just didn't feel like she had time for schoolwork.

After her resource room teacher noticed that she wasn't handing in a lot of her homework assignments, Sarah told her about her problem with finding time to do the work. After that, Sarah and her resource room teacher created a schedule. It showed all the days of the week and the times she had between getting home from school and her bedtime. Sarah and her teacher wrote in all the time slots that were not available for homework because she was busy with something like soccer practice or family dinner time. Next, they added the times when Sarah felt that she had to have social time. After putting in all of the things Sarah felt were priorities, Sarah noticed that she still had an hour and a half free each night. Her resource room teacher asked her to keep half an hour of that time for relaxation. That still left Sarah with one hour every night to do schoolwork. Sarah liked using this schedule. Except when something unusual happened, like a music recital at school, Sarah focused on doing homework each night. She felt prouder and more confident. Sarah was glad that now she was organized and no longer procrastinated.

Here are tips for learning how to avoid procrastination:

- Remember that you can feel relief and even pride when you take on tasks rather than trying to avoid or forget about them.

- Remind yourself that you will probably feel *more* anxiety or stress if you wait until the last minute to study or do a project.

- Being organized helps you figure out what to do now and what to do later. That helps you avoid last-minute panic.

- If it's hard for you to think about doing a large project, try starting with just a small step of the assignment.

- If you have a friend who is an expert on getting work done on time, talk with him or her about becoming study buddies.

Ingredient #4: Speaking Up for Yourself

Speaking up for yourself is also called **self-advocacy**. It means asking for information or help when you need it. Imagine sitting in class, feeling confused, and just putting your head down on the desk in defeat. This is definitely *not* speaking up for yourself.

In school, you can speak up for yourself by asking teachers for help if you need it. Another way to be a self-advocate is by being involved in your special education plan. **It is important for you to try the ideas your team comes up with.** But if you don't understand parts of the plan, or if you want to add something to the plan, it's also important to ask questions and respectfully share your thoughts. Think about Jin's story on the next page.

Jin is 10 years old. His Committee on Special Education (CSE) wrote his IEP to help him reach his goals more comfortably. They recommended that he go to the resource room for 40 minutes each day. There, his special education teacher goes over lessons that will be taught soon in his main class. This way, Jin can learn some of the material, or preview it, before learning the information in the larger group setting. Jin knows that his resource room time is useful. He told his grandpa, "I used to get overwhelmed and upset in class. When my teacher goes through material quickly, I have a hard time listening and understanding. I know I'm smart. But I learn better when my resource room teacher talks to me and just a few other kids. I get to ask lots of questions. Plus, she helps me learn in a way that matches my learning style."

Jin knew what his goals were in the resource room. He also knew how his special education teacher was going to try to help him reach his goals. Jin learned all of this information when he joined his IEP meeting. At that meeting, his team discussed his skills and his needs. Jin spoke up, too. He had written down what he felt he was good at and also what help he wanted. In addition, Jin asked a few questions when he didn't understand what a teacher said. Because he attended and spoke up at his meeting, Jin had a better understanding of his plan and knew that he was part of creating it.

Jin was a self-advocate because:

- He worked hard to focus and learn schoolwork.

- He understood that resource room was helping him. In the resource room, he sometimes asked questions about work that confused him.

- He was part of his IEP meetings. He helped the team figure out what support he needed and how much time he should spend in the resource room to receive it.

Sometimes, being an advocate for yourself means asking if you still need the help your team recommends. Other times, speaking up for yourself means asking for *more* help. It always means you are thinking about what you really need. You share what you need with others in a calm, respectful, and specific way.

School is not the only place where you can speak up for yourself. You can speak up in many places and at many times. Imagine your friend tells a joke that hurts your feelings. Speaking up for yourself means you respectfully tell your friend how you feel. You ask her to avoid jokes like that in the future. Your friend might even be glad that you spoke up, since she didn't mean to hurt you in the first place. Because you spoke up, it helped her know not to make similar jokes in the future.

Speaking up for yourself might also mean asking your parents to consider requests. For example, maybe you want to have a later bedtime, and you give your parents reasons for your request. When you

> **Speaking up respectfully lets others know what you want and what you need.**

speak up, you may not always get what you hope for. But your parents will know what you're feeling and what you want. And if you show that you are able to handle disappointment when you don't get what you want, it will be a sign that you are ready for these discussions again in the future. That will encourage your parents to listen the next time you share your thoughts. This time you may convince them that your request is fair and appropriate.

Sometimes it can be scary to be a self-advocate. But it's still important to try. People who speak up for themselves are often happier because they share their opinions and know that other people are listening to their questions and concerns. They know that **it's okay to speak up to get help to reach goals or to feel better.**

Here are some tips for speaking up for yourself:

- Know what you need and share this with others.

- Be clear and specific about what you need. For example, you might tell your teacher, "I need help pronouncing the names of these people for my oral report in social studies." This is clearer than, "I can't do my history report."

- Find the right time and place to talk about your needs. Choose a situation where the other person can really listen and respond. For example, rather than talking to your dad about an issue while he's trying to make dinner, wait until after the meal when he's not so busy.

- Be respectful and calm. Try not to get angry or argumentative. Listen carefully to what other people think about your needs and your requests.

- If you don't already go to your team meetings, think about attending one. Talk with your teachers or parents about whether it's possible for you to join a meeting or help make your school plan.

Ingredient #5: Self-Confidence

This ingredient for success is very important. **Self-confidence** is when you feel good about yourself. Self-confident people can laugh at their mistakes and also enjoy their successes. They are better able to try again after a challenge or a disappointment. They focus on their strengths and work hard to improve the things that are hard for them. And they enjoy being themselves. Does this describe you?

If you have self-confidence, it's also easier to take **healthy risks.** We often think that all risks are dangerous or bad. Some risks definitely are not healthy. For example,

Shari is 11 years old. She looked up to her older brother. He loved skateboarding and could do special tricks on the skateboard. Shari wanted to impress her brother. She thought that she would feel great about herself, and improve her self-confidence, if she surprised her brother with her ability to skateboard. So Shari went into her brother's room and took his skateboard. But she left his kneepads and helmet behind. She went outside and tried some of the advanced skateboarding skills she had seen her brother do. Guess what happened? Within a few minutes, Shari had fallen several times and her knees were scraped and scratched. Her confidence did not improve and her brother was not impressed.

Shari took an unhealthy risk. Healthy risks are different. You still might feel a little uneasy about something you have never tried before. But with healthy risks, you know that what you're doing is safe and that you can ask others for instructions or guidance. You can tell yourself, "I like who I am. And I can admit that I need help learning some things." Taking healthy risks means that you feel good enough about being you that you want to try new experiences that will not be harmful and that may be fun or give you new skills.

If you need help building self-confidence, try these ideas:

• Take time to feel good about your accomplishments. Congratulate yourself for working to meet your goals. Remind yourself of all your talents and abilities.

• Remember that no one is perfect. So it's okay if you have some challenges. Everyone does.

• Act as nice to yourself as you would to your best friend. Think nice thoughts about yourself. Say nice things to yourself.

> **Feeling confident doesn't mean you are perfect. It means that you still like yourself even when you are having trouble with something.**

If you still struggle to feel good about yourself, talk to a grownup you trust. He or she might be able to help you think of ways to feel better about being you. Or this grownup might arrange for you to meet with an expert to talk about your feelings. Experts who specialize in helping kids feel better include psychologists, psychiatrists, and social workers. They are trained to help people build self-confidence and other important skills.

Ingredient #6: Positive Self-Talk

Positive self-talk is a great way to help you feel good about yourself. Do you ever insult yourself? At first, you may think, "Why would anybody do that?" But it actually happens a lot.

Seth & Shantelle

Seth is 12 years old. After getting a disappointing test grade, he thought, "I'm so stupid!" **Shantelle** is 13 years old. After forgetting her friend's birthday, she thought, "I'm a horrible friend." Seth and Shantelle were being unkind to themselves. They were telling themselves negative information about themselves. This is also called negative self-talk. Negative self-talk often leads to decreased self-confidence, embarrassment, and even anger at yourself.

On the other hand, *positive* self-talk helps you feel good. It works even when you make a mistake. If Seth used positive self-talk, he might have said to himself, "I'm not happy with this grade. But I know I can do better. I'll talk to my resource room teacher and figure out what I did wrong this time. That way I won't make the same mistakes again." Seth's positive self-talk included a plan to speak up for himself by asking for help. He also believed that he could do better in the

> **Be as kind to yourself as you are to your best friend. Use positive self-talk.**

future. If Shantelle used positive self-talk, she might have said, "I'm usually a really good friend. But I really messed up big time. I'll tell my friend how sorry I am. And I'll make her a special card. I never made this mistake before. I don't think I'll ever make it again. I'm very thoughtful. I'll make it up to my friend." Shantelle gave herself a compliment. She also thought of ideas for making it up to her friend.

What about you? **Can you turn negative self-talk into positive self-talk?** Here are some tips for doing this:

- Try stating what went wrong and what you learned from it.
- State what you will do differently in the future.
- Avoid using negative words. (For example, "I'm so stupid!")
- Remind yourself that no one is perfect. So if you mess up, it just shows that you are human. And if you learn from the situation, it shows that you are wise.

Ingredient #7: Staying Motivated

Being **motivated** means you have the energy and interest to keep working toward a goal. It's often easier to feel motivated to do things that come easily to you and that you enjoy doing. But what happens when you struggle to finish some work? How can you stay motivated then?

One way to keep motivated is to give yourself rewards for what you accomplish. You, your teacher, or your parents may set up a point system. You may get points for doing certain tasks or chores. When you earn a certain number of points, you get a reward.

Rewards need to be realistic. It's probably *not* realistic to go on vacation after writing an essay! So think about what tasks you need to work on or complete in order to earn points. You and an adult should spend time discussing this, since not all rewards are possible in all settings. It's also important to decide how many points you need to earn before getting a reward. Consider what rewards would be reasonable and also a treat for you. Here are a few rewards other kids have used:

- taking a 10-minute break from studying to play a video game

- being a line-leader for a day when your class moves from one room to another

- getting a chance to make a classroom poster about staying motivated or one of the other skills you're learning

- having a friend sleep over

- getting a later bedtime for two nights

- having lunch on the weekend with a relative

Ramon is 9 years old. You read about him in Chapter 4. Ramon struggled with reading but loved to bake. After talking with his special education teacher and his mother, Ramon created a plan for helping him stay motivated. He read out loud to his mother each evening. If he read for 15 minutes, then his mother gave him a sticker and he put it on his sticker board. If he read for 25 minutes, he got two stickers. Once Ramon reached his goal of getting 10 stickers, he was able to pick a dessert from a cookbook and make it with his grandmother. Ramon was excited to earn stickers, and that helped him stay motivated while reading.

Once you figure out what motivates *you*, share it with your parents or teachers. Then you can work with them to think of ways to use this information to motivate you to do something that you find challenging or stressful.

As you think about these ideas, you may want to make a list of rewards that would help motivate you. Then check the list with your parents (or your teacher if you would receive the reward at school) to make sure they are okay with your ideas before you start working toward any of these rewards. If you all agree that the list is realistic, put it somewhere you can see it often. You might also **write down some positive self-talk ideas** and put them near your list. For example,

Staying motivated can give you the energy to focus on challenges.

you might write, "I feel good about myself when I work hard." You can look at your reward list and your positive statements whenever you need a boost of motivation.

Here are some other tips for staying motivated even when it's difficult:

- Think back to times when you worked hard and achieved your goals. Remind yourself how great that felt. This can motivate you to feel that way again now.

- Break up the work into smaller steps that you can finish pretty quickly. This helps you feel good about the progress you're making.

- Realize that the more work you do now, the less you have to do later.

- Remind yourself that the more motivated you can stay, the more likely you are to succeed.

Ingredient #8: Knowing How to Relax

It's important to chill out sometimes. No one can work on difficult tasks every minute of the day. And when we feel overwhelmed or stressed, we may be less able to focus on what we are supposed to be doing. We also may be less

Relaxation can be as important as working hard to help you do your best.

likely to remember what we are reading or studying. Have you noticed that you are able to listen to your teacher better when you are relaxed? If you answered yes, you aren't alone. Many kids have had similar experiences.

To help you relax and refocus, think of some fun activities that put a smile on your face or help you calm down.

You might want to make a list of things that you enjoy doing. You can look at the list when you need to de-stress. Here are a few ways other kids relax:

- listening to music
- dancing
- drawing
- hanging out with friends or family
- reading quietly
- playing a sport
- taking time for a hobby
- going for a walk or a run
- playing with a pet

Mae is 11 years old. She receives special education help in school and discovered that this support helps when she is working on her reading and writing skills. Mae knows that one of her talents is in music. She often receives compliments on how she plays the flute. When her flute teacher at school gave Mae and the other students a difficult piece to learn, he told them, "We'll go over this for the next month. There are some great skills you can learn by studying this musical piece."

Mae came home from school that day and started practicing the new piece right away. She realized that it was more difficult than other music that she has played. She practiced and practiced. When she kept making mistakes, she got angry with herself. When her mother told her to take a break for dinner, Mae shouted, "No! I need to get this. Maybe I really stink at the flute. I should just quit."

Mae didn't want to talk about it anymore. But she and her mother agreed that Mae would come to the dinner table within the next 15 minutes. Mae felt upset that she was struggling. As dinner got closer, she put more and more pressure on herself to play the piece perfectly. Instead, Mae started making more and more mistakes.

Mae was still frustrated and upset when she joined the rest of the family for dinner. But halfway through the meal, Mae realized that she was laughing and enjoying the conversation. She wasn't feeling tense anymore. Before Mae went back upstairs to practice some more, her mother gave her some ideas for staying relaxed. Here are the tips that Mae's mother gave her:

- Breathe deeply and slowly.
- Picture doing a relaxing activity. (For example, Mae could imagine herself painting, which she loved to do.)
- Use positive self-talk. (For example, Mae could remind herself that she is talented at the flute but this piece of music is difficult and will take time to learn.)
- Focus on a relaxing memory.
- Talk to someone if it's really hard to stay calm. (For example, if Mae felt that practicing was still not leading to improved skills, she could talk to her music teacher.)

Mae decided to just try to play the first page of the piece that night. She didn't put any pressure on herself. She wrote down a question for her teacher about one section she was struggling with. At the same time, she realized that she was playing other sections better now that she wasn't stressed.

There is no one right way to relax. You may want to try strategies similar to the ones that helped Mae. Some kids like to use relaxation exercises, such as thinking calm thoughts, picturing a favorite place, or breathing slowly in through the nose and out through the mouth. If you aren't sure what would work for you, ask your friends, family, or teachers how they relax.

Quick and Helpful Hints

In this chapter, you read about eight key ingredients that can help you be more successful, do well, and feel good. These ingredients can help you feel more confident and in control at school. They can also help you feel less stressed as you handle expectations and responsibilities. They can help you get your work done in school, and they can also help you at other times when you face new or challenging situations.

Here are the big ideas from this chapter:

- Perseverance is usually good, but if you keep trying a strategy that doesn't work, it's time for a new plan.

- Being organized may take extra time at first. But in the long run, it will actually save you time.

- Procrastinating won't make challenges disappear. So it's best to deal with responsibilities sooner, not later.

- Speak up if you aren't sure how to do something. Be specific about what is confusing you so another person can help you.

- Feeling good about yourself, even if you don't instantly understand how to do a task, can make learning much less stressful.

- Using positive self-talk is like having your best friend near you, reminding you to be kind to yourself and not to get down.

- Staying motivated can make completing a project or studying easier and more fun.

- Finding time to relax helps you stay calm and focused rather than stressed and overwhelmed.

In the next chapter, you will read about how to plan for your future. You will also read about what being in special education can mean for you as you move on in school.

Do You Already Have Some of These Special Skills?

Read the following sentences and put a check mark next to the ones that already describe you. Later, you may want to look back on how you responded to these items. Congratulate yourself on skills you have, and focus on areas that you want to work on.

○ When things are hard for me, I don't give up.

○ When I run into challenges, I'm not afraid to ask for help.

○ I try to start my work and my projects early. That way I don't have to rush through them at the last minute.

○ I have a system that works for remembering what homework I need to do.

○ I generally feel good about being me.

○ If I make mistakes, I know that I can still feel good about being me.

○ I mostly stay pretty organized.

○ When I feel stressed, I know how to relax and refocus.

○ If I have a project to do or have to study for a big test, I know how to stay motivated.

○ I remind myself of things I am doing to succeed, such as spending time studying.

CHAPTER 8

Thinking About the Future

Y ou have learned that special education is all about getting the education that is right for you. It means that you will be taught tools and given the support you need to succeed. It *doesn't* mean that you will only have a few choices for what you can do when you are an adult. However, **everyone needs to think about their strengths and their challenges when they make decisions about the future.** This is true for you and for all other kids. It is true when you are picking classes for high school. And it's also true when you start thinking about what jobs you might enjoy and what jobs might be right for you.

If you sometimes feel worried or nervous about your future, you are not alone. Everyone needs extra help at some time. If you already know your areas of strength, areas that you need help with, and how to ask for help, that's great. But some students who get special education worry about whether they will be able to do the work in high school. They may wonder if they can get extra help when they are in higher grades. This chapter will help you figure out how to make high school an enjoyable and comfortable learning environment. This chapter will also help you think about your future after high school. But before reading more of this chapter, turn to pages 152–153 and respond to the statements and questions there.

Teaching New Teachers About You

As you have gone through school, your teachers have probably learned a lot of ways to help you with schoolwork. They maybe even helped you with developing friendships or dealing with social situations. Hopefully, you have learned a lot about yourself, too. But what happens when each school year ends? You need to start over the next year with new teachers. They probably won't know much about you yet.

At the start of a school year, some teachers ask parents to write letters describing their children. Teachers want to know about the kids who will be in their classes. Your teacher may or may not do this. Either way, you can share with your teacher what you know about yourself and how you learn. **This is a chance to tell your teacher what it's like being you—both in and out of school.**

If you want, you can talk with your parents about writing a letter to your teacher. You may want to ask your parent to type what you'd like to say. It can be hard to keep track of everything you want to say and also focus on typing or writing it down. Cindy asked her dad to help her with her letter.

Cindy is 10 years old. Here is the letter that she asked her dad to type and send to her new teacher:

"Hello, Mr. Hoffman. My name is Cindy and I'm one of your new students. I want to tell you about me. I love swimming and hanging out with my friends. I have lots of friends because I'm funny and love to do many different things. I also play volleyball and play the piano. You need to know that I have an IEP. I got the IEP in second grade because I have a hard time with spelling and reading. I get resource room help, but I don't want to miss any fun stuff in your class when I'm out of the room. Last year, I had a different list of spelling words that were right for me. That helped me learn some of the spelling rules better. My resource room teacher this year is Mrs. Marshall and she knows me from last year. She can also tell you what I need. I learn better when my desk is near the board. And I can do better on tests when I have extra time to read the instructions and answer questions. Okay? See you soon!"

Think about what Cindy said in her letter.

- She showed she was polite by saying hello and introducing herself.
- She told her new teacher about her interests.
- She explained what she needs help with.
- She explained what kind of help works best for her.
- She shared that she knows about her own IEP.
- She described some things her teacher can do to help support her.

Now it's your turn. What do you want to tell your new teacher about yourself? Think about what you are proud of, what you like, and what you have trouble with. Teachers love getting to know about kids. But remember that they also know a lot about how different kids learn and what can help them. So tell your teacher about you!

Thoughts and Feelings About Your Future

Thinking about the future can be exciting. But it can also be scary to think about what might happen as you get older. How do you feel about your future? For example, maybe you have thought about how schoolwork will get harder in the higher grades. How do you feel about that?

Diego is 12 years old. When he went into sixth grade, he was really scared about his future. His older sister was in ninth grade. Diego had heard her say that the work she did was "super hard." He told his mom, "I might as well drop out of school now. I'll *never* be able to do the work in ninth grade. I can't even do the work now without help from my resource room teacher." Diego's mom listened to his feelings. Then she suggested meeting with the resource room teacher to talk about these worries. She thought that the teacher would have good ideas for how Diego could feel better.

The resource room teacher gave Diego a list of ideas and questions to think about. Diego learned a lot about himself by thinking about the items on this list.

Take a look at the following questions and think about your own answers.

- Think back to kindergarten. When you were little, something like writing three words may have taken a lot of effort. How did you feel when you reached this goal?

- Now imagine that your kindergarten teacher had told you that in third grade you would be writing paragraphs and taking spelling tests. How would you have felt learning about this back then? Would you have been nervous about the future and about going to third grade? Would you have been worried you would not be able to do the work? How do you feel *now* about these tasks that you started to do back in third grade? Even if they aren't easy for you, are they less scary than they would have been in kindergarten?

- Now, imagine being two years old and being told you had to make a poster showing what you know about insects. Yikes!

- Next, think about being thirteen years old and being told you need to learn enough about insects to make a poster. Hmm . . . that might even be fun, especially if you like the topic.

How do you feel after thinking about these ideas? Remembering how much progress he'd already made helped Diego. He saw that it's natural for people to feel nervous about doing work they are too young for or have not learned yet. Diego also felt better when he learned that if he needs resource room help in higher grades, he can get it.

In life, there is usually someone who can help you when you are struggling. Remember, asking for help when you need it is a smart, strong thing to do. That was true when you were younger. And it will still be true when you are older.

Looking Ahead to High School

It's normal to think about what your high school work will be like. But try not to worry about knowing everything right now. After all, no one expects you to write papers on subjects you've never learned or to take tests for classes you have never taken! Instead, focus on using and strengthening the skills you learned about in Chapters 6 and 7. That is one good way to prepare for the future.

At the same time, it's okay to admit that you have concerns. In fact, it can help to share your worries. Here was Penelope's experience.

Penelope is 16 years old. When she was 11, she told her teacher that she was worried about going to middle school. Penelope said, "If I need all this extra help to get through fifth grade, I'm never going to be able to do harder work." Do you have similar fears? If so, you may be relieved to know that you're not alone. Lots of kids are nervous about being able to do the work in the upper grades.

Penelope's teacher, Mrs. Diaz, said, "I love that you are thinking ahead. I don't want you to worry, though. If you do need help next year, your special education team will make sure you get it. They'll find help that is right for you. And you will have this help all the way through high school if you need it."

Penelope is in eleventh grade now. She went back to visit Mrs. Diaz. She told Mrs. Diaz, "I was thinking about what you told me before I left elementary school. You were right! I still get some special education help and I'm doing really well in classes. A lot of my friends are still working on remembering to study for tests and hand in projects on time. But I have no trouble with that. The organizational tips I learned from you help a lot. I'm taking some really challenging classes, just like my friends. It's true that some-times my tests have word banks so I don't have to remem-ber all the vocabulary. But the tests still measure how much I know."

Once you get to high school, you may notice that kids take a few different paths. Penelope was focused on whether she would be successful in her classes. She knew that having time for resource room would be helpful to her. That was the right addition to her schedule to make high school less stressful and more rewarding. But kids may also consider other options and ideas for high school years. Here are some of them:

- Some kids focus on taking academic classes like math, science, and English.

- Some kids take lots of academic classes but also make time for classes like art, fashion, music, or woodshop. These kids may want to do jobs someday related to these classes. Or they might just enjoy learning about these subjects or skills.

- Some students may be in the high school for only part of the day. Then they might go to another building to learn about specific work such as how to become a chef.

- Many kids, no matter how they spend their school time, volunteer after school or on weekends. They may do things such as visit elderly people, stock food shelves, or tutor younger students. These activities help others. But they can also help kids learn more about what they like to do and what they are good at.

What type of path do *you* want to follow? **Think about how you want to spend your time in and out of school.** Then talk all this over with your parents, teachers, or other grownups you trust. These are important choices.

Thinking About Life After High School

Have you thought about what you might want to do after you graduate from high school? If not, that's okay. But it can be fun to think about what to do in the future. Here are a few of the many possibilities you might consider:

- Going to a two-year college or a four-year college. At these schools, students focus on areas that they want to specialize in, such as chemistry, art, computers, or writing. The area a student focuses on is called a **major.**

- Getting a job after graduating from high school. (Some types of jobs require college, but others do not. Depending on what you are interested in or want to do, you may or may not need to go to college.)

- Going to a trade school and learning how to do a specific job. For example, electricians or mechanics may go to schools like this. These schools are also called **vocational schools** or **technical schools**.

- Becoming an apprentice. An apprentice learns how to do a job by getting some training and then spending time learning from an expert. For example, if you were interested in plumbing, you might become an apprentice to an experienced plumber.

- Joining the military. Some people who do this save money for a few years and go to college later. Others get training in certain skills and go on to get jobs using these skills. Other people have long careers in the military.

There are many possible paths. **Over time, you will get a better idea of the right path for you.** As you think about what you might do, it can be helpful to think about what you like, how you learn, and what talents you have. Maybe adults have told you that you can do anything you set your mind to. Parents and other grownups in your life probably want you to have dreams for your future. They want you to work toward goals that are important to you. That's a good thing! At the same time, it's important to know that no one is good at *everything*. When you think about your future, consider:

- your abilities

- your areas of difficulty or challenge

- your personality

- your interests

- your likes and dislikes

What kinds of goals are good matches for your personality? If you go to college, what would you be interested in studying? What jobs or careers would match up with your abilities? Read Charlotte's story on the next page.

Charlotte is 17 years old. When she started high school, she really wanted to be a professional dancer. Her dream was to perform in Broadway shows in New York City. So she took dance classes. But she hated all the time she had to put into practicing. Charlotte realized that dancing on a Broadway stage sounded fun, but she didn't really want to do all the work that it required. She also wasn't sure she was as talented as some of the other dancers in her classes.

Charlotte decided to look at other careers that might be a better fit for her. She was a talented artist who devoted hours and hours to drawing and painting. She also loved the theater. Charlotte ended up working at a small theater near her home, drawing and painting on the stage walls for shows. One of the directors saw her talent and suggested that she think about becoming a set designer for theater productions.

Charlotte's decision has nothing to do with the fact that she went to a resource room in school. Instead, it is based on her personality and what she knows about her own strengths and challenges.

What about your own goals, strengths, and challenges? Most students graduating from high school or college hope to get good jobs eventually. There are many kinds of jobs. And no one is a good match for every job. When you start thinking about what you want to do, choosing from the long list of possibilities may seem difficult. But it can also be interesting and enjoyable.

As you go through middle school and high school, remember to make some time to talk with your guidance counselors. They can help you think about your classes now and about your future. They can also give you tips for deciding what you might want to do after high school. You don't have to figure this out all by yourself.

Your counselors may have some fun forms or tests to help you think about these ideas. For example, the forms might include questions like, "Do you like to be around people or prefer to be alone?" These tests are often called **vocational assessments** or **career assessments**. They can give you ideas of what jobs people with your interests, personality, and strengths have enjoyed. If your counselors don't offer vocational assessments, they will have other ways to help guide you as you look toward your future.

Is There Only One Path to Success?

As you consider all of the possibilities for your future, remember that being in special education does not mean that you will always need help. It doesn't mean that you can't go to college. And it definitely does not mean that you can't get a job you like as an adult. Read about Andrew's experience on the next page.

Andrew is 25 years old. When he was finishing college, he wanted to work with his father. His father was a journalist and wrote articles for a popular newspaper. The problem was, Andrew had trouble with spelling and grammar. Andrew's father told him, "I would love to work with you and have you nearby every day. But I'm not sure *you* would enjoy having to work extra hard on writing all the time. You are really talented in math and science. Remember how much you loved learning about genetics? Why not talk to your career counselor about jobs in math or science?"

Years later, Andrew was talking with his dad one night when they had dinner together. He thanked his dad for the great advice his dad had given years earlier. Andrew had become a math teacher. He worked at a middle school. He told his dad, "I love my job. I'm good at it, too. You were right to suggest that I consider jobs other than journalism. I found the right path for me. Thanks!"

Andrew's job choice was good for him for several reasons. He enjoyed math and he was good at it. He also found out that he had a real talent for *teaching* math. He liked working with teenagers. And he was outgoing and enjoyed talking in front of the class.

It's important to know that there is no one right path to success. And your path doesn't have to go a certain way just because you're in special education. You can also change your path. If you go to a college that ends up not being the right place for you, or you start working in a job that doesn't turn out like you hoped, it's okay to consider changing your path. Talk to people you trust. Don't feel stuck without speaking up.

You have big decisions ahead of you, and that's exciting. You don't have to know exactly what you want yet. And you can change your mind as you get older and learn even more about yourself. **You have choices—and that's great!**

Quick and Helpful Hints

In this chapter, you learned that you have a lot of options for your future. The path you take may depend on what you enjoy, what your strengths and challenges are, and how hard you want to work in a certain area. Remember to ask lots of questions. Talk to family members, teachers, and even friends. Ask about the many interesting kinds of school, work, and other possibilities you can explore.

Here are some important things to keep in mind from this chapter:

- Just because you have some challenges in school does *not* mean that you will have fewer choices in life. Your future is full of opportunities.

- There is no one path to being successful. That's good news!

- You don't have to figure out your future path by your-self. You can turn to people at school and outside of school for guidance.

Remember that being in special education means that you get help learning in a way that works for you. It doesn't mean that you can't succeed. In fact, it *helps* you succeed. And your attitude makes a big difference. **If you believe you can do well in life, you are more likely to do well.** So use the tools in this book to help yourself stay positive and feel good about yourself now—and in your future.

How Do You Feel About Your Future?

Read the following sentences. Which ones describe you? Mark *yes* if the sentence describes you and *no* if it does not yet describe you.

1. I feel ready for school next year. ○ YES   ○ NO

2. I know my schoolwork will get more challenging each year. But I am confident that I'll be ready for it as I get older. ○ YES   ○ NO

   If you answered no, write about what is worrying you. Then, share your worries with a trusted adult.

   _____

   _____

3. I feel comfortable asking for extra help in the future, even when I'm in high school or college. ○ YES   ○ NO

   If you answered no, write down why you are uncomfortable about asking for help. Then share these reasons with a trusted adult.

   _____

   _____

4. I know how to ask adults for support so they know what I need help with. ○ YES   ○ NO

5. I know how to teach my teachers about who I am and about my strengths and challenges.   ◯ YES   ◯ NO

If you answered no, who can you ask for help with this?

_____

_____

6. If I need more or different help as I go into a new grade, I know that I can share this opinion with my team at my Committee on Special Education or my 504 meeting.   ◯ YES   ◯ NO

7. I know that as an adult I will be able to find a job that is right for me.   ◯ YES   ◯ NO

8. I know that I can use my abilities and talents to help me succeed.   ◯ YES   ◯ NO

Write down some of those abilities, talents, and strengths here.

_____

_____

9. I know that these strategies can help me now and in the future: remaining calm, asking for help when I need it, and being open to new ways of learning.   ◯ YES   ◯ NO

A Note to Parents

As a parent, you know that raising a child is more than a full-time job. You probably also have found it to be one of the most rewarding opportunities a person can have. However, if your child is not growing or gaining skills as expected, you may be wondering where and to whom you can turn for guidance.

Whatever your worries are—and whether you are just beginning to seek information or your child already receives special education—you may have silently experienced emotions that are common when parents know or suspect that their child is having difficulties.

Take some time to think about your worries regarding your child's progress. Once you have had a chance to explore your feelings, you will be better able to take additional steps toward helping your child. It's also helpful to be very specific about your concerns so you know how to express them to others. Then, make a list of these concerns. Hold onto the list for a few days to make sure you thought of everything you are worried about. Do you have a partner, friend, or person in your community who you can talk with and gain support from? It's often helpful to share concerns so that you don't feel like you're dealing with them on your own.

The next step is to learn how to find and access the right resources to help your child succeed, now and in the future.

Getting the Right Help

The resources you might seek for your child will depend on the nature of your child's needs. For example, your concerns may fall into one of these developmental categories:

- speech and language (speaking, writing, and understanding language)

- gross motor skills (balance, large motor movements, and coordination)

- fine motor skills (handwriting and visual tracking)

- cognition (learning, recalling, and thinking)
- age-appropriate independence skills (tying shoes, brushing hair, and feeding oneself)

When you know the specific nature of your child's challenges, you will have a better idea of what help or advice is needed. Resources can include support from professionals such as pediatricians, neurologists, optometrists or ophthalmologists, ENT doctors, psychologists, psychiatrists, or other experts trained to help children. Other support may come from your child's school, community support groups, other parents and caregivers, or community agencies that might be able to guide you in your search for the correct expert to help your child. You may also find valuable information in books, journals, and online resources.

If you seek professional help for your child, be prepared to describe your child's behaviors, language skills, and social skills. If the professionals you see want information on your child's skills on a standardized measure, they may recommend one of these tests (or additional tests specific to their specialty): psychological evaluation; educational evaluation; speech/language evaluation; physical therapy evaluation; occupational therapy evaluation; auditory processing evaluation; vision evaluation; audiological evaluation; assistive technology evaluation; or reading evaluation. Testing may reveal (or may already have revealed) that your child has strengths but also has areas of difficulty. Evaluators may give you some activities to try at home to help your child improve in certain skill areas. At other times, services within the school might be available.

Next Steps

Depending on where you and your child are in your special education journey, you may be surprised and relieved to learn that schools must follow state and federal government regulations and guidelines when a child is believed to have a significant difficulty that could impact him or her in school. Local education boards in public schools also have policies that must be in accordance with state and federal laws.

Two very important federal laws address the needs of students in special education: the Individuals with Disabilities Education

Act (IDEA) and Section 504 of the Rehabilitation Act of 1973 (under the Americans with Disabilities Act). These laws include a lot of technical language that can be overwhelming if you are not a lawyer or an educator. But practically speaking, the laws translate into teams of people at your school who will support your child. (They will help support you as a parent, too.) Depending on your child's needs, the teams may include a school-based support team, a Committee on Special Education (CSE), or a 504 team (sometimes called a Section 504 Team or 504 Committee).

THE SCHOOL-BASED SUPPORT TEAM

Most often, the first group of people to monitor children who struggle in some part of their school day is the *school-based support team*. This team is likely to step in after the classroom teacher tries various support techniques. This team may be called something different in your school district, such as the Instructional Support Team, Child Study Team, Intervention Specialists Team, or the Consultation Team. This team generally meets on a regular basis, and teachers can set up times to meet with the team to discuss students in their classes whom they are concerned about.

This multidisciplinary team may include the following people:

- a principal or other school administrator
- a reading specialist
- a special education teacher or learning specialist
- a speech-language therapist or pathologist
- an occupational therapist
- a physical therapist
- a psychologist
- a social worker
- a general education teacher
- any other professional who may have knowledge of your child or have expertise in the issues being discussed

Because circumstances vary based on each student's needs, the job of the school-based support team may also vary. This group does not have a cookie-cutter approach to exploring the needs of children. Instead, team responses are tailored to the needs of each student. The team will likely review all of the information the school currently has available, such as teacher reports, report cards, standardized test scores, and informal assessments. The team might also review information you have shared about your child, including your concerns and observations, relevant medical information, or evaluations done outside of school. The school-based support team may then make recommendations such as:

- continuing to monitor your child's progress

- administering assessments or other testing

- providing building-level services such as math help, reading help, or help with articulation

- making a referral to a more specialized team such as the Committee on Special Education or the 504 team

THE COMMITTEE ON SPECIAL EDUCATION AND THE 504 TEAM

Depending on your child's needs, he or she may be eligible for specific help beyond the school-based support team. This help may be provided through the Committee on Special Education or the 504 team. These two teams have many similarities. The school will help determine (based in part on the federal laws) which committee is the right one to help your child.

The Committee on Special Education (often referred to as a CSE) is a legally mandated group. Because of this mandate, very specific requirements govern who needs to attend meetings, although these requirements vary somewhat from state to state. In general, however, the professionals who attend CSE meetings will have direct knowledge of your child or the issues of concern, and will be knowledgeable about the services the school can offer.

The CSE's main goal is to determine if your child has one or more disabilities drawn from a specific list, and if these disabilities are impacting his or her ability to learn in the classroom. If so, the CSE will also work to determine what your child needs in order to succeed within the school setting. The CSE then creates an Individualized Education Program (IEP) unique to your child.

This document can be updated at any time, but an annual review is required. This review determines how the IEP may need to be revised, or if your child still needs a plan.

Similar to the CSE, the 504 team is governed by federal regulations. The 504 team's job is to determine if your child has a disability or an impairment that substantially limits one or more major life activities, including your child's ability to learn or function in school. Also similar to the CSE, people who are knowledgeable about your child or about the condition of concern will discuss ways to help your child function more easily during the school day. If your child is eligible under Section 504, the team will develop an annual plan (called a 504 Plan) to define what services your child will receive. This plan can be reviewed and edited if changes need to be made before a year has elapsed.

PARENTS' RIGHTS AND ROLES AT TEAM MEETINGS

At CSE or 504 meetings, parents may initially be unsure about their roles and what questions to ask. First, it's important to know that you, as a parent, are a key member of your child's team, and you have the right to attend these meetings. When you take part in these meetings, you may find it helpful to prepare a list of questions and comments beforehand. Your questions and comments might include:

- Based on testing, what will my child need extra help with? What goals is he working to reach?

- Will my child miss class time to get these services? If so, will she fall behind because she's not in the room for the lessons?

- How do I explain this extra help to my child?

- What can I do at home to help my child?

- I have noticed that my child struggles with _____. Will this be addressed at school?

Types of Support

When your child's CSE or 504 team has been assembled, their first task is to decide whether your child is eligible to receive a tailored plan through the team. If your child's needs are minimal or can be addressed with building-level supports, the team will likely refer you back to the teacher (and perhaps a specific contact person in the building) for guidance on what support will be given. However, if your child meets eligibility through the CSE or 504, then part of the team's job is to create your child's educational plan and determine which services are recommended. These recommendations will be based on the results of your child's evaluations, and the experience and expertise of team members—including you.

The team may recommend one or more services, such as:

- resource room help
- consultant teacher (For instance, this person may consult with the classroom teacher on how to offer lessons so your child's learning needs can be considered. Or, a consultant teacher may meet with your child or come into the classroom to help.)
- testing accommodations
- changes to schoolwork or homework
- other changes, such as to class size, desk placement, or daily schedule (For example, a child who has walking issues may leave class a few minutes early to get to the next room before the hallway gets crowded with other students.)
- assistive technology (For example, some computer programs can help children who struggle with writing. Students can also do math work online or talk into a computer to transcribe speech.)
- staff education for certain topics or programs (For instance, if your child has seizures, the nurse may educate key staff members on what to do if a seizure occurs.)
- counseling
- speech or language therapy
- occupational therapy
- physical therapy
- vision therapy

When fewer services are recommended, it generally means the team thinks your child can succeed in the typical educational setting with minimal support. When more services are provided, the team believes your child would benefit from intervention or changes to multiple areas of his or her school plan. The committee's goal is to give your child the support he or she needs to succeed, while also leaving room for your child to work on being independent.

You should only proceed with a support plan when your questions have been answered and you understand what this plan will look like for your child.

Responding to a Special Education Recommendation

Parents of children who receive special education services may have many feelings about the process, the future, and much more. Many parents feel worried, afraid, angry, overwhelmed, disappointed, frustrated, or hopeless—especially at the beginning of the special education process. Some parents struggle with sadness realizing that their child is not just going through a stage but truly requires specialized help. Other parents experience concern because they believe that life may be more difficult for their children.

On the other hand, some parents feel relief at understanding their child's specific difficulties and knowing that he or she is receiving appropriate help. Additionally, many parents report feeling less isolated when they learn that other parents have had similar concerns and found ways to help their children. If you still feel isolated, speak up. Ask to talk with the special education staff members who are helping your child. See if your school offers a special education parent group that you can join.

You will likely experience many ups and downs along this journey, as you move toward acceptance and also help your child navigate through obstacles. In addition, now that you know your child has a challenge requiring extra help, and as you learn more about that difficulty, you probably also realize that you are not in control of making things better. All children will face some stress and pain as they grow—whether they receive special education or not. It can help to remember that some stress can have a positive effect for a child. Stress provides an opportunity to develop resilience. Confronting challenges can help children build confidence and coping skills as they learn to overcome or work around difficult times. Of course, overwhelming stress is problematic. If you feel that your child is overwhelmed, contact the team to see how to further support your child so that goals are within reach and not just creating frustration.

Sharing Information with Your Child

There is no one right way to talk to your child about his or her strengths, needs, and challenges. Over time, it does become helpful for a child to know his strengths and weaknesses. However, sharing specific numbers from evaluations—such as IQ test results or reading scores—may be confusing for some children. Sharing this data might even backfire. A child who excelled may be less motivated to work, while a child who received a low score may feel defeated. Specific details may also cause children to feel defined by their scores, or to believe that they will always be "stuck" at a certain level. This type of information, especially IQ scores, may not help children understand what they need help with. In fact, many experts believe that children do not need these numbers to progress or understand themselves. However, other information—such as a child's learning style—may be useful in educating your child on how he or she can best learn and succeed. And it *is* important for you, as the parent, to know why specific tests are needed and what they mean. If you have questions, check in with your child's teachers or other members of the school team.

If you feel unsure about how much to tell your child, you may want to ask his or her team for advice. Remember, though, that you can't "unshare" information, so think carefully before discussing scores and similar data. Whatever details you decide to share, be sure to talk with your child about how special education will help him or her more easily reach his or her goals, and that it is a chance to build valuable skills that will help throughout his or her life.

Keeping the lines of communication open with children is important as they grow, develop, and have new thoughts or intense feelings. This is true for all children. For children who have special needs, they may need you to model for them how to start conversations about their feelings or their self-perceptions and needs. It can be helpful to read this entire book, or key portions, with your child and use the text as a starting point for discussions.

Giving Your Child Space to Grow

It's natural for parents to want to do whatever they can to help their children. And it is important for you to be an advocate for your child. At the same time, it's essential to realize that setting certain boundaries is important. Without these boundaries, parents may accidentally upset or embarrass their child or even accidentally communicate to their child that he can't succeed without constant adult intervention. For example, consider the experience of Susan, whose daughter Malia is 10 years old and who has a learning disability in reading. Susan was passionate about being a caring advocate for her daughter. She read a lot about reading challenges and went to many conferences on the topic.

One day, Susan went to the school and met with Malia and her resource room teacher. In an attempt to support her daughter, Susan told the teacher, "Malia *could* learn, but you aren't teaching her the right way." Susan then listed teaching strategies that *she* recommended. Malia left the room in tears.

Malia later told the school psychologist, "My mom embarrassed me so much. She must think I'm a total idiot if I can't learn from my teacher. And she doesn't seem to think my teacher is doing a good job, either. But I really like my resource room teacher. And I thought I was doing better in my work. I'm so confused."

Susan had good intentions, but in her attempt to help Malia, she did not trust Malia's team or listen to why the experts had chosen certain educational plans for her. Susan also did not notice that the strategies in place were already helping and that Malia was feeling good about her progress.

With Malia's permission, the school psychologist shared this information with Susan. After their discussion, Susan was able to acknowledge that it wasn't productive for her to fight everyone in an attempt to help her daughter. She realized that Malia had a caring support team and that she was learning great strategies for coping with her challenges and succeeding at school and beyond. Malia and her mother had a long talk at home. Malia felt empowered and relieved after this discussion.

A few points of caution: If you're reteaching all of your child's work to her during homework time, it's helpful to share this information with the teacher. Otherwise, the teacher may not realize that your child is struggling with the work. Or, if you aren't sure why specialists are setting certain goals for your child, organize a meeting with your child's team, and come to that meeting open to learning and discussion. If you feel that you want to be the sole helper of your child, take a breath. It's okay to acknowledge that your role as parent is special and has a tremendous impact on your child. But it's also important to recognize the benefit of having a team of specialists, each working in their own designated area of expertise.

Empowering Your Child and Focusing on Abilities

As you and your child navigate the special education system, you can empower your child and help him or her cope with both the struggles and successes he or she will face. This process may include:

- guiding her on figuring out when to rely on herself and when to ask for help

- helping him learn the patience and perseverance to try certain tasks independently

- encouraging her to clearly see, understand, and consider her own strengths and challenges

- helping him find ways to speak up for himself and explain his needs to others

Another important goal that you as a parent can focus on is shining a spotlight on your child's strengths, talents, and abilities. As you probably know, there is no one right way to feel and no feelings are wrong. However, if a parent worries about how a child will be able to function because of his or her disability, the child may pick up on these concerns. Children are sensitive to moods and feelings. They often pick up on more than we realize. So while it's okay to acknowledge the challenges your child faces, it's essential that you also remember to focus on his or her strengths. No matter how much energy you put into helping your child compensate for, overcome, or deal with difficulties, it's just as important to make time to focus on his or her unique and positive qualities. If you consistently communicate that your child has abilities, your child may display more self-confidence, be more willing to work on weaknesses, and be more open to believing that he can succeed in life. In other words, if you show that you appreciate your child, your child is more likely to appreciate himself or herself. You are a mirror that helps your child see his or her own reflection and value.

In addition to conveying your appreciation for your child through everyday words and actions, you may want to sit down with your child and create a list of his or her positive qualities. This can be a fun activity and can help your child focus more on strengths and talents, while also acknowledging the challenges. Some children keep their lists in their rooms and look at them when they need a boost in spirits.

As you support your child through the special education process and find the appropriate support for him or her, also remember to work on building his or her executive functioning skills. These skills are critical when a person (adult or child) is trying to take on a new challenge, manage many responsibilities, or improve in an area. They include:

- confidence
- perseverance
- flexible thinking
- attention to details
- time management
- organization
- self-advocacy

You can foster these skills in many different ways. Be creative. See what works for you and your family. Helping your child keep an organized desk space and use a monthly calendar to keep track of assignments and tests can be useful in building organizational skills and avoiding procrastination. For time management, some children struggle with figuring out how long tasks might take. Before starting homework, your child can estimate how long it will take him to complete the math homework. Then, set a timer—not for rewards or to speed up his work, but to show him how long that task actually took. Teachers can also guide you on what home supports you might be able to institute to help your child develop these skills.

With this foundation, your child is more likely to grow into a confident teenager and adult. She will be more likely to take on the world with a positive attitude and set realistic and rewarding goals. While you may wish you could always guide your child and minimize the obstacles that she may encounter, one of the greatest gifts you can give your child is the confidence and skills to manage obstacles and challenges independently. As you continue to think about how best to support and empower your child, consider these wishes, which we have heard expressed by many children in special education:

- Children want to know what strategies they can use when they feel frustrated, sad, or overwhelmed so that they can feel more positive and self-confident.

- Children want to understand themselves.

- Children want to be able to accept themselves—challenges and all.

- Children want to know that *others* understand and accept them.

Looking to the Future

Have you thought about what your primary role is for your child— especially with an eye to the future? Some of your goals as a parent may be to give your child opportunities, fun times, laughter, and a sense of being loved. All of these things are important. But take some time to think about the following additional goals:

- Preparing your child to navigate the world and the obstacles he may encounter.

- Teaching your child healthy coping strategies. (For example, encouraging her to ask for guidance if homework is difficult rather than giving up or having a tantrum.)

- Helping your child understand that he can seek out support from others, even as an adult, to help him navigate challenges.

- Reminding your child that no one is perfect, and that it's okay to make mistakes and still feel good about herself.

Each child is unique. You may want to think about your wishes for your child. Then, see if your wishes can come true. Some wishes sound great but aren't practical or even useful. For instance, wanting your child to never struggle sounds wonderful, but some struggles may help your child gain confidence to handle life's challenges as he or she gets older. If your number one wish is to have a confident child, think about whether you need guidance in instilling this attitude. If so, others may be able to help you reach this goal. Perhaps a mental health professional, a relative, a friend, or a teacher might have good tips for you. Just as it's important for your child to speak up and ask for help when necessary, it's also crucial for you to seek the support and expertise you need.

Remembering to Take Care of Yourself

Before concluding, it's important to mention that it's okay to focus on yourself sometimes. In fact, it's essential. When you take care of yourself, you are better able to take care of your child and handle what is ahead. So remember to pay attention to your own emotions and energy. You will then be in a better position to support, nurture, and advocate for your child. We wish you well on this journey.

Resources for Kids and Adults

A Bad Case of Stripes by David Shannon (Scholastic Inc., 1998). This book for younger readers uses colorful illustrations to explore the idea that, even though kids sometimes change or hide who they are just to fit in, it's okay to think differently or to be different in some way.

Being Me: A Kid's Guide to Boosting Confidence and Self-Esteem by Wendy L. Moss, Ph.D. (Magination Press, 2011). This book helps kids focus on their abilities and feel confident in school, with friends, and in simply being themselves.

Center for Parent Information and Resources
parentcenterhub.org
Every state is required to have a parent technical assistance center. This site helps parents connect with their local region and provides information specific to supports and services provided for students with disabilities.

Child Development Institute
childdevelopmentinfo.com
This website presents information on a variety of topics for parents (of children with and without special needs). Materials include blogs, articles, and links to other resources such as books and organizations supporting children and parents.

Fish in a Tree by Lynda Mullaly Hunt (Nancy Paulsen Books, 2015). This novel tells Ally's story. She is a whiz at math, but she has trouble with reading. She hid her challenges all through elementary school. But when she gets to middle school, one of her teachers gives Ally the help she needs.

National Center for Learning Disabilities
ncld.org
Parents, professionals, educators, and young adults with disabilities can all find helpful information on this site. A section on advocacy discusses various laws in user-friendly language.

PACER Center
pacer.org
The PACER Center is dedicated to helping children and young adults
with disabilities, as well as their families, and helping them achieve
their potential in life. The website presents a range of resources on
relevant topics.

*School Made Easier: A Kid's Guide to Study Strategies and Anxiety-Busting
Tools* by Wendy L. Moss, Ph.D., and Robin A. DeLuca-Acconi, LCSW
(Magination Press, 2014). This book explores the stress that students
may feel when faced with schoolwork and offers ways to reduce
anxiety. This book also explores tips and techniques for coping with
academic expectations.

*Stick Up for Yourself! Every Kid's Guide to Personal Power and Positive
Self-Esteem* by Gershen Kaufman, Ph.D., Lev Raphael, Ph.D., and
Pamela Espeland (Free Spirit Publishing, 1999). An excellent resource
for kids about learning and building assertiveness skills.

Too Perfect by Trudy Ludwig (Tricycle Press, 2009). This picture book
explains how wanting to be perfect is a lot of pressure and not a
reachable goal, but trying hard and feeling good about yourself can
lead to greater happiness—and even more success.

Understood
understood.org
This website is the joint project of numerous nonprofit organizations
and brings together resources specifically for parents and caregivers
of kids with learning and attention challenges.

U.S. Department of Education
ed.gov/parents/needs/speced/edpicks.jhtml
This website presents an overview of special education from birth
through college, including info on student loans, students' rights,
guidance on regulations, and current data and research studies.

Index

About the Authors

Wendy L. Moss, Ph.D., ABPP, FAASP, has over 30 years of experience working with children and families as a psychologist in schools, clinics, hospitals, and private practice. She earned her doctorate in clinical psychology, is a certified school psychologist, and has been appointed as a fellow in the American Academy of School Psychology. She has also been awarded the status of a "Diplomate in School Psychology" by the American Board of Professional Psychology. Dr. Moss is the author of six books, including *Being Me: A Kid's Guide to Boosting Confidence and Self-Esteem.* She lives in the New York City area.

Denise Campbell, M.S., has enjoyed a dynamic career as a speech pathologist and later as a school district administrator. Over the years, she has conducted evaluations and provided instructional services to hundreds of children and developed positive relationships with families. She has worked with children affected by a myriad of disabilities. She is the proud parent of five wonderful children, and in her spare time, she enjoys reading, cooking, and camping. She lives in the New York City area.

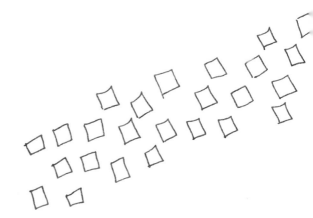

Other Great Books from Free Spirit

The Survival Guide for School Success
Ron Shumsky, Susan M. Islascox, and Rob Bell
For ages 10–14.

The Survival Guide for Making and Being Friends
James J. Crist, Ph.D.
For ages 8–13.

The Survival Guide for Kids with Behavior Challenges
Tom McIntyre, Ph.D.
For ages 9–14.

The Survival Guide for Gifted Kids
Judy Galbraith
For ages 10 & under.

The Survival Guide for Kids with ADHD
John F. Taylor, Ph.D.
For ages 8–12.

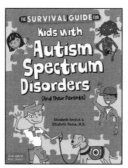

The Survival Guide for Kids with Autism Spectrum Disorders (And Their Parents)
Elizabeth Verdick and Elizabeth Reeve, M.D.
For ages 9–13.

The Survival Guide for Kids with LD
Rhoda Cummings, Ed.D.
For ages 9–14.

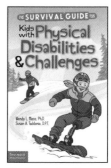

The Survival Guide for Kids with Physical Disabilities & Challenges
Wendy L. Moss, Ph.D., and Susan A. Taddonio, D.P.T.
For ages 8–13.

Find all the Free Spirit SURVIVAL GUIDES for Kids at www.freespirit.com/survival-guides-for-kids